Elict
27)47
www.eapl.org

31241007384020

OCT -- 2011

Nutrition

Other Books of Related Interest:

Opposing Viewpoints Series

Agricultural Subsidies

Obesity

Water

At Issue Series

Anorexia

Can Diets Be Harmful?

Food Safety

Is Organic Food Better?

The Local Food Movement

Should Junk Food Be Sold in Schools?

Current Controversies Series

Factory Farming

The Global Food Crisis

Vegetarianism

"Congress shall make no law . . . abridging the freedom of speech, or of the press."

First Amendment to the US Constitution

The basic foundation of our democracy is the First Amendment guarantee of freedom of expression. The *Opposing Viewpoints* series is dedicated to the concept of this basic freedom and the idea that it is more important to practice it than to enshrine it.

OPPOSING
VIEWPOINTS®
SERIES

Nutrition

David Haugen and Susan Musser, Book Editors

GREENHAVEN PRESS
A part of Gale, Cengage Learning

GALE
CENGAGE Learning™

Detroit • New York • San Francisco • New Haven, Conn • Waterville, Maine • London

GALE
CENGAGE Learning·

Elizabeth Des Chenes, *Managing Editor*

© 2012 Greenhaven Press, a part of Gale, Cengage Learning.

Gale and Greenhaven Press are registered trademarks used herein under license.

For more information, contact:
Greenhaven Press
27500 Drake Rd.
Farmington Hills, MI 48331-3535
Or you can visit our Internet site at gale.cengage.com

ALL RIGHTS RESERVED.
No part of this work covered by the copyright herein may be reproduced, transmitted, stored, or used in any form or by any means graphic, electronic, or mechanical, including but not limited to photocopying, recording, scanning, digitizing, taping, Web distribution, information networks, or information storage and retrieval systems, except as permitted under Section 107 or 108 of the 1976 United States Copyright Act, without the prior written permission of the publisher.

For product information and technology assistance, contact us at

Gale Customer Support, 1-800-877-4253
For permission to use material from this text or product, submit all requests online at www.cengage.com/permissions

Further permissions questions can be emailed to permissionrequest@cengage.com

Articles in Greenhaven Press anthologies are often edited for length to meet page requirements. In addition, original titles of these works are changed to clearly present the main thesis and to explicitly indicate the author's opinion. Every effort is made to ensure that Greenhaven Press accurately reflects the original intent of the authors. Every effort has been made to trace the owners of copyrighted material.

Cover Image copyright Ocean/Corbis.

LIBRARY OF CONGRESS CATALOGING-IN-PUBLICATION DATA

Nutrition / David Haugen and Susan Musser, book editors.
    p. cm. -- (Opposing viewpoints)
    Includes bibliographical references and index.
    ISBN 978-0-7377-5751-4 (hardcover) -- ISBN 978-0-7377-5752-1 (pbk.)
    1. Nutrition--United States. 2. Food--United States. I. Haugen, David M., 1969- II. Musser, Susan.
    TX360.U6N8363 2011
    613.20973--dc23
                                                                    2011017997

Printed in the United States of America
1 2 3 4 5 6 7 15 14 13 12 11

Contents

Chapter 3: What Societal Factors Influence Nutrition?

Chapter 4: What Personal Nutrition and Dietary Choices Impact Health?

Why Consider
Opposing Viewpoints?

> *"The only way in which a human being
> can make some approach to knowing the
> whole of a subject is by hearing what
> can be said about it by persons of every
> variety of opinion and studying all
> modes in which it can be looked at by
> every character of mind. No wise man
> ever acquired his wisdom in any mode
> but this."*
>
> *John Stuart Mill*

In our media-intensive culture it is not difficult to find differing opinions. Thousands of newspapers and magazines and dozens of radio and television talk shows resound with differing points of view. The difficulty lies in deciding which opinion to agree with and which "experts" seem the most credible. The more inundated we become with differing opinions and claims, the more essential it is to hone critical reading and thinking skills to evaluate these ideas. Opposing Viewpoints books address this problem directly by presenting stimulating debates that can be used to enhance and teach these skills. The varied opinions contained in each book examine many different aspects of a single issue. While examining these conveniently edited opposing views, readers can develop critical thinking skills such as the ability to compare and contrast authors' credibility, facts, argumentation styles, use of persuasive techniques, and other stylistic tools. In short, the Opposing Viewpoints Series is an ideal way to attain the higher-level thinking and reading skills so essential in a culture of diverse and contradictory opinions.

In addition to providing a tool for critical thinking, *Opposing Viewpoints* books challenge readers to question their own strongly held opinions and assumptions. Most people form their opinions on the basis of upbringing, peer pressure, and personal, cultural, or professional bias. By reading carefully balanced opposing views, readers must directly confront new ideas as well as the opinions of those with whom they disagree. This is not to simplistically argue that everyone who reads opposing views will—or should—change his or her opinion. Instead, the series enhances readers' understanding of their own views by encouraging confrontation with opposing ideas. Careful examination of others' views can lead to the readers' understanding of the logical inconsistencies in their own opinions, perspective on why they hold an opinion, and the consideration of the possibility that their opinion requires further evaluation.

Evaluating Other Opinions

To ensure that this type of examination occurs, *Opposing Viewpoints* books present all types of opinions. Prominent spokespeople on different sides of each issue as well as well-known professionals from many disciplines challenge the reader. An additional goal of the series is to provide a forum for other, less known, or even unpopular viewpoints. The opinion of an ordinary person who has had to make the decision to cut off life support from a terminally ill relative, for example, may be just as valuable and provide just as much insight as a medical ethicist's professional opinion. The editors have two additional purposes in including these less known views. One, the editors encourage readers to respect others' opinions—even when not enhanced by professional credibility. It is only by reading or listening to and objectively evaluating others' ideas that one can determine whether they are worthy of consideration. Two, the inclusion of such viewpoints encourages the important critical thinking skill of objectively evaluating an author's credentials and bias. This evaluation will illuminate an author's reasons for taking a particular stance on an issue and will aid in readers' evaluation of the author's ideas.

It is our hope that these books will give readers a deeper understanding of the issues debated and an appreciation of the complexity of even seemingly simple issues when good and honest people disagree. This awareness is particularly important in a democratic society such as ours in which people enter into public debate to determine the common good. Those with whom one disagrees should not be regarded as enemies but rather as people whose views deserve careful examination and may shed light on one's own.

Thomas Jefferson once said that "difference of opinion leads to inquiry, and inquiry to truth." Jefferson, a broadly educated man, argued that "if a nation expects to be ignorant and free . . . it expects what never was and never will be." As individuals and as a nation, it is imperative that we consider the opinions of others and examine them with skill and discernment. The *Opposing Viewpoints* series is intended to help readers achieve this goal.

David L. Bender and Bruno Leone,
Founders

Introduction

"Our kids aren't hungry because we lack food or because of a lack of food and nutrition programs. They are hungry because they lack access to programs that provide the nutritious food they need to grow and thrive."

—Timothy Cipriano,
executive director of food services,
New Haven Public Schools

"The way we feed our children today will dictate the country we have tomorrow."

—José Andrés,
principal, ThinkFoodGroup

In July 2010 the Education and the Workforce Committee of the US House of Representatives passed the Improving Nutrition for America's Children Act. The bill is aimed chiefly at improving school breakfast and lunch programs. It calls for schools to revise menus based on updated nutrition standards and requires that all foods offered through vending machines or other outlets on school grounds meet these standards. The act also seeks to expand school meal programs to feed more children of low-income families and provide them with nutritious foods they might not get at home. First Lady Michelle Obama and a host of lawmakers, nutrition experts, and even celebrities supported the bill's broader passage in the House and hoped that it would spur passage of a similar bill in the Senate. The House recessed in October 2010 before voting on the legislation, but the Senate's Healthy, Hunger-Free Kids Act—which proposed comparable changes—was signed into law in December.

Supporters of the two bills pushed for their passage because they feared any postponement would mean that many children in America would go another year without healthy food. Secretary of Agriculture Tom Vilsack testified before the House committee that any delay would suggest that "we are not doing right by our kids." As most of the witnesses appearing before the committee argued, America's children are not being raised on healthy foods and are not being taught how to make healthy food choices. Some speakers brought up grim statistics that indicated poor food choices had led the country into an obesity epidemic that was severely impacting children. Eduardo Sanchez, the vice president and chief medical officer for Blue Cross and Blue Shield of Texas, pointed to the Trust for America's Health report *F as in Fat: How Obesity Policies Are Failing America 2009*, which claims that more than one-third of US children aged ten to seventeen are obese or overweight. Sanchez told the committee that "some experts warn that if obesity rates continue to climb, today's young people may be the first generation in American history to live sicker and die younger than their parents' generation." He concluded by asserting that "the health of America's children depends on a prescription for healthy food and more physical activity."

While Sanchez and other congressional witnesses showed concern over the fate of America's future generations, many health experts have warned that the nation as a whole has been suffering from the consequences of poor nutrition. The report by the Trust for America's Health, for example, clearly states that obesity is not simply a problem for the young. Obesity rates among adults in America have doubled since 1980, the health organization maintains. While the causes of obesity are varied, the trust cites food choices as one contributory factor. The report draws a correlation between states with high obesity rates and a low percentage of adults who consume the recommended two to three servings of fruits and vegetables per day. It also claims that there may be some relation between high poverty rates and high obesity rates in specific states, suggesting that the high cost of healthy foods may be pricing them off the tables of poor families.

Inexpensive food has often been targeted as a source of weight gain, and the principal culprit many point to in America is corn. The overproduction of corn in the United States has led to the crop being used as feed for beef cattle and other livestock as well as the source of high-fructose corn syrup, a sweetener that has been added to everything from soda to spaghetti sauce to bread. In a February 18, 2004, article on SFGate.com, Carol Porter, director of nutrition and food services at the University of California, San Francisco Medical Center, is quoted as stating, "It's not that fructose itself is so bad, but they put it in so much food that you consume so much of it without knowing it." Kim Severson, the *San Francisco Chronicle* writer who penned the piece, then points out that "a single 12-ounce can of soda has as much as 13 teaspoons of sugar in the form of high-fructose corn syrup." Some researchers, though, dismiss the connection between corn sweetener and obesity. In a July 2, 2006, *New York Times* column, Walter Willett, the chairman of the nutrition department at the Harvard School of Public Health, told staff writer Melanie Warner, "There's no substantial evidence to support the idea that high-fructose corn syrup is somehow responsible for obesity." He and other quoted experts attested that corn sweeteners have not been proven to be any worse nutritionally than white sugar. Whether or not diets high in corn syrup yield significant weight gain, the debate has prompted some Americans to begin reading ingredient labels to understand the nutritional content of the foods they are consuming. On September 8, 2010, Bidisha Mandal published a report in *Consumer Affairs* that argued food purchasers who routinely read food labels had better results in maintaining a healthy weight than those who did not. However, reading food labels must become a priority for Americans if the supposed benefits are to accrue to those who have a wealth of food choices.

In other parts of the globe, nutrition and weight gain are also becoming pressing concerns for those who for decades have been burdened by food insecurity. The United Nations Food and Agriculture Organization (FAO) has begun charting the dangers of modern food distribution to developing countries. Improving economies and expanding trade have given developing nations more food choices and access to higher calorie diets from industrialized nations. The FAO website cautions that "traditional diets featuring grains and vegetables are giving way to meals high in fat and sugar." The organization states that obesity goes hand in hand with these dietary changes. "Even sub-Saharan Africa, where most of the world's hungry live, is seeing an increase in obesity," the FAO asserts. The World Health Organization (WHO) raised the alarm in the 1990s that global trends in obesity were reaching epidemic proportions. WHO experts insist that teaching nutrition is the way to combat weight gain, but the number of global citizens who are clinically obese has topped three hundred million since 2000.

In *Opposing Viewpoints: Nutrition*, experts and commentators explore the links between food production and obesity, as well as other concerns regarding dietary choices. In chapters titled How Has Nutrition Changed as a Result of Modern Food Production? What Should Be Done to Improve Nutrition and Fight Obesity? What Societal Factors Influence Nutrition? and What Personal Nutrition and Dietary Choices Impact Health? the authors debate the impact of nutritional choices on personal health and social well-being. Some look for causes of a supposed decline in concern for nutrition, while others caution that overreaction may not lead to better health. Looming over these debates is the question of whether legislation like the Healthy, Hunger-Free Kids Act can make a difference in choices that seem personal. *Opposing Viewpoints: Nutrition* addresses these issues and examines how public discussion and individual choice are shaping the health of nations.

How Has Nutrition Changed as a Result of Modern Food Production?

Chapter Preface

In the early nineteenth century, British economist Thomas Malthus began warning of an impending catastrophe—a situation in which human population growth would outpace the ability of societies to produce sufficient amounts of food to feed their populations. In the ensuing decades, scientists heeded Malthusian warnings and began developing agricultural techniques to ensure sufficient global production of nutritious foods. These experiments culminated with the efforts of American agronomist Norman Borlaug who developed and exported new farming techniques to the developing world to fend off hunger in what became known as the "Green Revolution." With the proliferation of selective plant breeding for certain climates and conditions combined with modern, large-scale farming methods that included the utilization of fertilizer, tractors, and modern irrigation methods, Borlaug's Green Revolution helped to feed millions around the world.

While the widespread adoption of these techniques has improved the nutritional intake of individuals in countries such as Mexico, India, and several in Africa, many critics argue that the widespread adoption of these advancements and the coinciding development of agricultural technology have resulted in unforeseen consequences that present new challenges to the health of people around the world. One of the most criticized new developments is the genetic modification of crops. In this process, scientists introduce non-plant-based gene material into plants in an attempt to improve a certain crop's resistance to potentially harmful herbicides or pests. Critics argue that this technique produces unnatural organisms with potentially harmful effects to humans. In a 2011 article in *Better Nutrition*, Melissa Diane Smith states that American Academy of Environmental Medicine research suggests "there are serious health risks associated with eating GM [genetically modified] foods, including infertility, immune system problems, accelerated aging, disruption of insulin and cholesterol regulation, gastrointestinal problems, and organ damage." Smith concludes that these risks do not justify the supposed advantages of genetically modified organisms (GMOs) such as increased crop yield and decreased pesticide use, and research has yet to confirm these benefits.

Even in the face of such criticism, many proponents of GMOs maintain that planting these crops in food insecure areas is safe, increases production, and improves the nutritional intake of populations. In an article in the journal *New Biotechnology*, Matin Qaim, an agricultural economist, assesses the advantages of the GM crop Golden Rice, which has been engineered to contain beta-carotene, a nutrient essential to controlling vitamin A deficiency. Vitamin A deficiency is common in rural Asia where the populations do not have access to nutrient-rich diets, but consume high quantities of rice. After reviewing the research concerning the crop, Qaim concludes, "Golden Rice has the potential to reduce the burden of vitamin A deficiency substantially and at low average costs . . . [and] promises to be an effective, efficient and sustainable pro-poor nutrition intervention." He criticizes objections to GM crops as the result of "biased information" and calls for "better and more science-based information flows" to combat these views.

The controversy over GM crops is only one facet of the larger debate concerning the impact of modern food production techniques on human health and nutrition. In the following chapter, various authors examine the impact of industrialized production and organic farming on nutritional intake and investigate whether hunger remains a problem in the modern world.

> *"All of our uncertainties about nutrition should not obscure the plain fact that the chronic diseases that now kill most of us can be traced directly to the industrialization of our food."*

Modern Industrialized Food Is Not Nutritious

Michael Pollan

The modern Western diet consumed by the majority of Americans is making people sick and fat, argues Michael Pollan in the following viewpoint. The components of this diet, he contends, are less healthful than the substances humans have consumed throughout history. He believes modern foods are now overprocessed, industrialized products that, while edible, are merely "foodlike." Pollan traces the rapid changes in the American diet using his own family as an example, telling how in the span of only one generation, dietary trends and eating habits shift multiple times. The author attributes these changes to marketing, nutrition science, and journalism that all combine to confuse and mislead the public about eating choices. Pollan calls on Americans to abandon the modern Western diet because he be-

Michael Pollan, *In Defense of Food: An Eater's Manifesto*, pp. 1–16. Copyright © 2008 by Michael Pollan. Used by permission of The Penguin Press, a division of The Penguin Group (USA) Inc.

lieves it is the cause of chronic diseases that plague the nation. Michael Pollan is a professor of journalism at the University of California, Berkeley and author of the books The Omnivore's Dilemma *and* The Botany of Desire.

As you read, consider the following questions:

1. According to Pollan, how did his mother's diet change over the course of her life, from her childhood to adulthood?

2. What are the three myths that Pollan states "nutritionism" has convinced people of?

3. What developments characterize the industrialization of food, as stated by Pollan?

Eat food. Not too much. Mostly plants.

That, more or less, is the short answer to the supposedly incredibly complicated and confusing question of what we humans should eat in order to be maximally healthy. . . .

Eating a little meat isn't going to kill you, though it might be better approached as a side dish than as a main. And you're better off eating whole fresh foods rather than processed food products. That's what I mean by the recommendation to "eat food," which is not quite as simple as it sounds. For while it used to be that food was all you *could* eat, today there are thousands of other edible foodlike substances in the supermarket. These novel products of food science often come in packages elaborately festooned with health claims, which brings me to another, somewhat counterintuitive, piece of advice: If you're concerned about your health, you should probably avoid products that make health claims. Why? Because a health claim on a food product is a strong indication it's not really food, and food is what you want to eat.

You can see how quickly things can get complicated. . . .

Unprecedented Changes in Diet

As omnivores—creatures that can eat just about anything nature has to offer and that in fact need to eat a wide variety of different things in order to be healthy—the "What to eat" question is somewhat more complicated for us than it is for, say, cows. Yet for most of human history, humans have navigated the question without expert advice. To guide us we had, instead, Culture, which, at least when it comes to food, is really just a fancy word for your mother. What to eat, how much of it to eat, what order in which to eat it, with what and when and with whom have for most of human history been a set of questions long settled and passed down from parents to children without a lot of controversy or fuss.

But over the last several decades, mom lost much of her authority over the dinner menu, ceding it to scientists and food marketers (often an unhealthy alliance of the two) and, to a lesser extent, to the government, with its ever-shifting dietary guidelines, food-labeling rules, and perplexing pyramids. Think about it: Most of us no longer eat what our mothers ate as children or, for that matter, what our mothers fed us as children. This is, historically speaking, an unusual state of affairs.

My own mother grew up in the 1930s and 1940s eating a lot of traditional Jewish-American fare, typical of families who recently emigrated from Russia or Eastern Europe: stuffed cabbage, organ meats, cheese blintzes, kreplach, knishes stuffed with potato or chicken liver, and vegetables that often were cooked in rendered chicken or duck fat. I never ate any of that stuff as a kid, except when I visited my grandparents. My mother, an excellent and adventurous cook whose own menus were shaped by the cosmopolitan food trends of New York in the 1960s (her influences would have included the 1964 World's Fair; [celebrity chef] Julia Child and [food writer and critic] Craig Claiborne; Manhattan restaurant menus of the time; and of course the rising drumbeat of food marketing) served us a rotating menu that each week completed a culinary world tour: beouf bourguignon or beef Stroganoff on Monday; coq au vin or oven-fried chicken (in a Kellogg's Cornflakes crust) on Tuesday; meat loaf or Chinese pepper steak on Wednesday (yes, there was a *lot* of beef); spaghetti pomodoro with Italian sausages on Thursday; and on her weekend nights off, a Swanson's TV dinner or Chinese take-out. She cooked with Crisco or Wesson oil rather than chicken or duck fat and used margarine rather than butter because she'd absorbed the nutritional orthodoxy of the time, which held that these more up-to-date fats were better for our health. (Oops.)

Nowadays I don't eat any of that stuff—and neither does my mother, who has moved on too. Her parents wouldn't recognize the foods we put on the table, except maybe the butter, which is back. Today in America the culture of food is changing *more* than once a generation, which is historically unprecedented and dizzying.

Food Science, Marketing, and Journalism Drive Dietary Shifts

What is driving such relentless change in the American diet? One force is a thirty-two-billion-dollar food-marketing machine that thrives on change for its own sake. Another is the constantly shifting ground of nutrition science that, depending on your point of view, is steadily advancing the frontiers of our knowledge about diet and health or is just changing its mind a lot because it is a flawed science that knows much less than it cares to admit. Part of what drove my grandparents' food culture from the American table was official scientific opinion, which, beginning in the 1960s, decided that animal fat was a deadly substance. And then there were the food manufacturers, which stood to make very little money from my grandmother's cooking, because she was doing so much of it from scratch—up to and including rendering her own cooking fats. Amplifying the "latest science," they managed to sell her daughter on the virtues of hydrogenated vegetable oils, the ones that we're now learning may be, well, deadly substances. . . .

The story of how the most basic questions about what to eat ever got so complicated reveals a great deal about the institutional imperatives of the food industry, nutrition science, and—ahem—journalism, three parties that stand to gain much from widespread confusion surrounding the most elemental question an omnivore confronts. But humans deciding what to eat without professional guidance—something they have been doing with notable success since coming down out of the trees—is seriously unprofitable if you're a food company, a definite career loser if you're a nutritionist, and just plain boring if you're a newspaper editor or reporter. (Or, for that matter, an eater. Who wants to hear, yet again, that you should "eat more fruits and vegetables"?) And so like a large gray cloud, a great Conspiracy of Scientific Complexity has gathered around the simplest questions of nutrition—much to the advantage of everyone involved. Except perhaps the supposed beneficiary of all this nutritional advice: us, and our health and happiness as eaters. For the most important thing to know about the campaign to professionalize dietary advice is that it has not made us any healthier. To the contrary . . . most of the nutritional advice we've received over the last half century (and in particular the advice to replace the fats in our diets with carbohydrates) has actually made us less healthy and considerably fatter. . . .

An Unhealthy Obsession with Healthy Eating

But if food and eating stand in need of a defense, from whom, or what, do they need defending? From nutrition science on one side and from the food industry on the other—and from the needless complications around eating that together they

The Ideology of Low Fat Takes Hold of America

Several developments that came together in the 1980s and 1990s help explain how the ideology of low fat conquered America in those decades. The dietary context was an established tradition of low-calorie, low-fat dieting for weight reduction that predisposed Americans to accept what was promoted as a heart-healthy diet. A plethora of diet-heart studies carried out by scientists and physicians suggested that a low-fat diet might prevent heart disease. These studies drew on research that had been done from the 1950s through the 1970s. By the late 1970s, the federal government started promoting the low-fat diet, and shortly thereafter the food industry began to make low-fat products available and to advertise them widely. Low-fat foods proliferated in the 1980s and 1990s, demonstrated by the number of products available in grocery stores and the ads that appeared in magazines and on television. Adhering closely to the published results of scientific research, the popular health press spread the low-fat message of the scientific/medical establishment and the federal government, supported the food industry, and informed consumers by carrying ads for low-fat foods.

Ann F. La Berge,
"How the Ideology of Low Fat Conquered America,"
Journal of the History of Medicine and Allied Sciences,
April 2008.

have fostered. As eaters we find ourselves increasingly in the grip of a Nutritional Industrial Complex—comprised of well-meaning, if error-prone, scientists and food marketers only too eager to exploit every shift in the nutritional consensus.

Together, and with some crucial help from the government, they have constructed an ideology of nutritionism that, among other things, has convinced us of three pernicious myths: that what matters most is not the food but the "nutrient"; that because nutrients are invisible and incomprehensible to everyone but scientists, we need expert help in deciding what to eat; and that the purpose of eating is to promote a narrow concept of physical health. Because food in this view is foremost a matter of biology, it follows that we must try to eat "scientifically"—by the nutrient and the number and under the guidance of experts.

If such an approach to food doesn't strike you as the least bit strange, that is probably because nutritionist thinking has become so pervasive as to be invisible. We forget that, historically, people have eaten for a great many reasons other than biological necessity. Food is also about pleasure, about community, about family and spirituality, about our relationship to the natural world, and about expressing our identity. As long as humans have been taking meals together, eating has been as much about culture as it has been about biology.

That eating should be foremost about bodily health is a relatively new and, I think, destructive idea—destructive not just of the pleasure of eating, which would be bad enough, but paradoxically of our health as well. Indeed, no people on earth worry more about the health consequences of their food choices than we Americans do—and no people suffer from as many diet-related health problems. We are becoming a nation of orthorexics: people with an unhealthy obsession with healthy eating.

The Western Diet Makes People Sick and Fat

I don't mean to suggest that all would be well if we could just stop worrying about food or the state of our dietary health: *Let them eat Twinkies!* There are in fact some very good reasons to worry. The rise of nutritionism reflects legitimate concerns that the American diet, which is well on its way to becoming the world's diet, has changed in ways that are making us increasingly sick and fat. Four of the top ten causes of death today are chronic diseases with well-established links to diet: coronary heart disease, diabetes, stroke, and cancer. Yes, the rise to prominence of these chronic diseases is partly due to the fact that we're not dying earlier in life of infectious diseases, but only partly: Even after adjusting for age, many of the so-called diseases of civilization were far less common a century ago—and they remain rare in places where people don't eat the way we do.

I'm speaking, of course, of the elephant in the room whenever we discuss diet and health: "the Western diet." . . . All of our uncertainties about nutrition should not obscure the plain fact that the chronic diseases that now kill most of us can be traced directly to the industrialization of our food: the rise of highly processed foods and refined grains; the use of chemicals to raise plants and animals in huge monocultures; the superabundance of cheap calories of sugar and fat produced by modern agriculture; and the narrowing of the biological diversity of the human diet to a tiny handful of staple crops, notably wheat, corn, and soy. These changes have given us the Western diet that we take for granted: lots of processed foods and meat, lots of added fat and sugar, lots of *everything*—except vegetables, fruits, and whole grains.

That such a diet makes people sick and fat we have known for a long time. Early in the twentieth century, an intrepid group of doctors and medical workers stationed overseas observed that wherever in the world people gave up their traditional way of eating and adopted the Western diet, there soon followed a predictable series of Western diseases, including obesity, diabetes, cardiovascular diseases, and cancer. They called these the Western diseases and, though the precise causal mechanisms were (and remain) uncertain, these observers had little doubt these chronic diseases shared a common etiology: the Western diet.

What's more, the traditional diets that the new Western foods displaced were strikingly diverse: Various populations thrived on diets that were what we'd call high fat, low fat, or high carb; all meat or all plant; indeed, there have been traditional diets based on just about any kind of whole food you can imagine. What this suggests is that the human animal is well adapted to a great many different diets. The Western diet, however, is not one of them.

The Consequences of the Western Diet Can Be Avoided

Here, then, is a simple but crucial fact about diet and health, yet, curiously, it is a fact that nutritionism cannot see, probably because it developed in tandem with the industrialization of our food and so takes it for granted. Nutritionism prefers to tinker with the Western diet, adjusting the various nutrients (lowering the fat, boosting the protein) and fortifying processed foods rather than questioning their value in the first place. Nutritionism is, in a sense, the official ideology of the Western diet and so cannot be expected to raise radical or searching questions about it.

But we can. By gaining a firmer grasp on the nature of the Western diet—trying to understand it not only physiologically but also historically and ecologically—we can begin to develop a different way of thinking about food that might point a path out of our predicament. In doing so we have two sturdy—and strikingly hopeful—facts to guide us: first, that humans historically have been healthy eating a great many different diets; and second, that, as we'll see, most of the damage to our food and health caused by the industrialization of our eating can be reversed. Put simply, we can escape the Western diet and its consequences. . . .

The Postindustrial Era of Food

You may well, and rightly, wonder who am I to tell you how to eat? Here I am advising you to reject the advice of science and industry—and then blithely go on to offer my own advice. So on whose authority do I purport to speak? I speak mainly on the authority of tradition and common sense. Most of what we need to know about how to eat we already know, or once did until we allowed the nutrition experts and the advertisers to shake our confidence in common sense, tradition, the testimony of our senses, and the wisdom of our mothers and grandmothers.

Not that we had much choice in the matter. By the 1960s or so it had become all but impossible to sustain traditional ways of eating in the face of the industrialization of our food. If you wanted to eat produce grown without synthetic chemicals or meat raised on pasture without pharmaceuticals, you were out of luck. The supermarket had become the only place to buy food, and real food was rapidly disappearing from its shelves, to be replaced by the modern cornucopia of highly processed foodlike products. And because so many of these novelties deliberately lied to our senses with fake sweeteners and flavorings, we could no longer rely on taste or smell to know what we were eating.

Most of my suggestions come down to strategies for escaping the Western diet, but before the resurgence of farmers' markets, the rise of the organic movement, and the renaissance of local agriculture now under way across the country, stepping outside the conventional food system simply was not a realistic option for most people. Now it is. We are entering a postindustrial era of food; for the first time in a generation it is possible to leave behind the Western diet without having also to leave behind civilization. And the more eaters who vote with their forks for a different kind of food, the more commonplace and accessible such food will become.

> "Modernism had provided what was
> wanted: food that was processed, pre-
> servable, industrial, novel, and fast, the
> food of the elite at a price everyone
> could afford."

Modern Industrialized Food Is Nutritious

Rachel Laudan

*Modern, industrialized foods have come under increasing criti-
cism in recent years as consumer preferences have shifted from a
focus on convenience to an obsession with the natural, organic,
traditional, and homemade. Many perceive this shift as a move
toward a healthier lifestyle; however, Rachel Laudan questions
the desire for all foods, natural and traditional, in the viewpoint
that follows. Laudan argues that this need to return to earlier
means of food production is a type of "Culinary Luddism," refer-
ring to the early nineteenth-century philosophy that rebelled
against progress through the use of industrial machinery. This
belief system, the author maintains, ignores the historical record,
which reveals that earlier eras did not consume more healthful
diets. Laudan urges everyone to develop a new understanding of*

Rachel Laudan, "A Plea for Culinary Modernism: Why We Should Love New, Fast, Processed Food," *The Gastronomica Reader*, University of California Press, 2010, pp. 280–
292. Copyright © 2010 by University of California Press. All rights reserved. Reproduced
by permission.

modern food that honestly assesses nutrition and convenience of new food production methods. Rachel Laudan is a historian who has written extensively about the intersection of food and science in publications such as Scientific American, Gastronomica, *and* Saveur.

As you read, consider the following questions:

1. As stated by the author, what are the dichotomies espoused by Culinary Luddites to give credence to their distaste for modern food?

2. What are some of the examples, given by the author, of the dangers humans have faced throughout history when eating?

3. How did societies change with the advent of modern food, according to the author?

Modern, fast, processed food is a disaster. That, at least, is the message conveyed by newspapers and magazines, on television cooking programs, and in prizewinning cookbooks. It is a mark of sophistication to bemoan the steel roller mill and supermarket bread while yearning for stone-ground flour and brick ovens; to seek out heirloom apples and pumpkins while despising modern tomatoes and hybrid corn; to be hostile to agronomists who develop high-yielding modern crops and to home economists who invent new recipes for General Mills. We hover between ridicule and shame when we remember how our mothers and grandmothers enthusiastically embraced canned and frozen foods. We nod in agreement when the waiter proclaims that the restaurant showcases the freshest local produce. We shun Wonder Bread and Coca-Cola. Above all, we loathe the great culminating symbol of Culinary Modernism, McDonald's—modern, fast, homogenous, and international.

The Rise of Culinary Luddism

Like so many of my generation, my culinary style was created by those who scorned industrialized food; Culinary Luddites, we may call them, after the English handworkers of the nineteenth century who abhorred the machines that were destroying their traditional way of life. I learned to cook from the books of [British food writer] Elizabeth David, who urged us to sweep our store cupboards "clean forever of the cluttering debris of commercial sauce bottles and all synthetic flavorings." . . . Today I rush to the newsstand to pick up *Saveur* with its promise to teach me to "Savor a world of authentic cuisine."

Culinary Luddism involves more than just taste. Since the days of the counterculture, it has also presented itself as a moral and political crusade. Now in Boston, the Oldways Preservation and Exchange Trust works to provide "a scientific basis for the preservation and revitalization of traditional diets." Meanwhile, Slow Food, founded in 1989 to protest the opening of a McDonald's in Rome, is a self-described Greenpeace for Food; its manifesto begins, "We are enslaved by speed and have all succumbed to the same insidious virus: Fast Life, which disrupts our habits, pervades the privacy of our homes and forces us to eat Fast Foods. . . . Slow Food is now the only truly progressive answer." As one of its spokesmen was reported as saying in the *New York Times*, "Our real enemy is the obtuse consumer."

At this point I begin to back off. I want to cry, "Enough!" But why? Why would I, who learned to cook from Culinary Luddites, who grew up in a family that, in Elizabeth David's words, produced their "own home-cured bacon, ham and sausages . . . churned their own butter, fed their chickens and geese, cherished their fruit trees, skinned and cleaned their own hares" (well, to be honest, not the geese and sausages), not rejoice at the growth of Culinary Luddism? Why would I (or anyone else) want to be thought "an obtuse consumer"?

Or admit to preferring unreal food for unreal people? Or to savoring inauthentic cuisine?

The answer is not far to seek: because I am a historian. As a historian I cannot accept the account of the past implied by Culinary Luddism, a past sharply divided between good and bad, between the sunny rural days of yore and the grey industrial present. My enthusiasm for the Luddites' kitchen wisdom does not carry over to their history, any more than my response to a stirring political speech inclines me to accept the orator as scholar. The Luddites' fable of disaster, of a fall from grace, smacks more of wishful thinking than of digging through archives. It gains credence not from scholarship but from evocative dichotomies: fresh and natural versus processed and preserved; local versus global; slow versus fast; artisanal and traditional versus urban and industrial; healthful versus contaminated and fatty. History shows, I believe, that the Luddites have things back to front.

The Desire for Natural Foods Is a Recent Phenomenon

That food should be fresh and natural has become an article of faith. It comes as something of a shock to realize that this is a latter-day creed. For our ancestors, natural was something quite nasty. Natural often tasted bad. Fresh meat was rank and tough, fresh milk warm and unmistakably a bodily excretion; fresh fruits (dates and grapes being rare exceptions outside the tropics) were inedibly sour, fresh vegetables bitter. Even today, natural can be a shock when we actually encounter it. When [French celebrity chef] Jacques Pépin offered free-range chickens to friends, they found "the flesh tough and the flavor too strong," prompting him to wonder whether they would really like things the way they naturally used to be.

Natural was unreliable. Fresh fish began to stink, fresh milk soured, eggs went rotten. Everywhere seasons of plenty were followed by seasons of hunger when the days were short, the weather turned cold, or the rain did not fall. Hens stopped laying eggs, cows went dry, fruits and vegetables were not to be found, fish could not be caught in the stormy seas. Natural was usually indigestible. Grains, which supplied from fifty to ninety percent of the calories in most societies, have to be threshed, ground, and cooked to make them edible. Other plants, including the roots and tubers that were the life support of the societies that did not eat grains, are often downright poisonous. Without careful processing, green potatoes, stinging taro, and cassava bitter with prussic acid are not just indigestible, but toxic.

Nor did our ancestors' physiological theories dispose them to the natural. Until about two hundred years ago, from China to Europe, and in Mesoamerica, too, everyone believed that the fires in the belly cooked foodstuffs and turned them into nutrients. That was what digesting was. Cooking foods in effect pre-digested them and made them easier to assimilate. Given a choice, no one would burden the stomach with raw, unprocessed foods.

So to make food tasty, safe, digestible and healthy, our forebears bred, ground, soaked, leached, curdled, fermented, and cooked naturally occurring plants and animals until they were literally beaten into submission. To lower toxin levels, they cooked plants, treated them with clay (the Kaopectate effect), and leached them with water, acid fruits and vinegars, and alkaline lye. They intensively bred maize to the point that it could not reproduce without human help. They created sweet oranges and juicy apples and non-bitter legumes, happily abandoning their more natural but less tasty ancestors. They built granaries for their grain, dried their meat and their fruit, salted and smoked their fish, curdled and fermented their dairy products, and cheerfully used whatever additives and preservatives they could—sugar, salt, oil, vinegar, lye—to make edible foodstuffs. . . .

"You may not feel any healthier right away, but you'll definitely feel more smug," by Mike Baldwin. www.CartoonStock.com.

A History of Processed, Fast, and Fried Foods

Processed and preserved foods kept well, were easier to digest, and were delicious: raised white bread instead of chewy wheat porridge; thick, nutritious, heady beer instead of prickly grains of barley; unctuous olive oil instead of a tiny, bitter fruit; soy milk, sauce, and tofu instead of dreary, flatulent soy beans; flexible, fragrant tortillas instead of dry, tough maize; not to mention red wine, blue cheese, sauerkraut, hundred-year-old eggs, Smithfield hams, smoked salmon, yogurt, sugar, chocolate, and fish sauce. . . .

As for slow food, it is easy to wax nostalgic about a time when families and friends met to relax over delicious food, and to forget that, far from being an invention of the late twentieth century, fast food has been a mainstay of every society. Hunters tracking their prey, fishermen at sea, shepherds tending their flocks, soldiers on campaign, and farmers rushing to get in the harvest all needed food that could be eaten quickly and away from home. The Greeks roasted barley and ground it into a meal to eat straight or mixed with water, milk, or butter (as the Tibetans still do), while the Aztecs ground roasted maize and mixed it with water to make an instant beverage (as the Mexicans still do). . . .

Deep-fried foods, expensive and dangerous to prepare at home, have always had their place on the street: doughnuts in Europe, *churros* in Mexico, *andagi* in Okinawa, and *sey* in India. Bread, also expensive to bake at home, is one of the oldest convenience foods. For many people in West Asia and Europe, a loaf fresh from the baker was the only warm food of the day. To these venerable traditions of fast food, Americans have simply added the electric deep fryer, the heavy iron griddle of the Low Countries, and the franchise. The McDonald's in Rome was, in fact, just one more in a long tradition of fast-food joints reaching back to the days of the Caesars. . . .

Eating Has Always Been Dangerous

Were old foods more healthful than ours? Inherent in this vague notion are several different claims, among them that foods were less dangerous, that diets were better balanced. Yet while we fret about pesticides on apples, mercury in tuna, and mad cow disease, we should remember that ingesting food is, and always has been, inherently dangerous. Many plants contain both toxins and carcinogens, often at levels much higher than in any pesticide residues. Grilling and frying add more. Some historians argue that bread made from moldy, verminous flour, or adulterated with mash, leaves, or bark to make it go further, or contaminated with hemp or poppy seeds to drown out sorrows, meant that for five hundred years Europe's poor staggered around in a drugged haze subject to hallucinations. Certainly, many of our forebears were drunk much of the time, given that beer and wine were preferred to water, and with good reason. In the cities, polluted water supplies brought intestinal diseases in their wake. In France, for example, no piped water was available until the 1860s. Bread was likely to be stretched with chalk, pepper adulterated with the sweepings of warehouse floors, and sausage stuffed with all the horrors famously exposed by [American author] Upton Sinclair in *The Jungle* [a novel showing the hardships of the working class and the squalid conditions of the meatpacking industry]. Even the most reputable cookbooks recommended using concentrated sulphuric acid to intensify the color of jams. Milk, suspected of spreading scarlet fever, typhoid, and diphtheria as well as tuberculosis, was sensibly avoided well into the twentieth century, when the United States and many parts of Europe introduced stringent regulations. My mother sifted weevils from the flour bin; my aunt reckoned that if the maggots could eat her home-cured ham and survive, so could the family. . . .

By the standard measures of health and nutrition—life expectancy and height—our ancestors were far worse off than we are. Much of the blame was due to the diet, exacerbated by living conditions and infections which affect the body's ability to use the food that is ingested. No amount of nostalgia for the pastoral foods of the distant past can wish away the fact that our ancestors lived mean, short lives, constantly afflicted with diseases, many of which can be directly attributed to what they did and did not eat. . . .

Industrialization of Food Saves People from Servitude and Starvation

Meanwhile, most men were born to a life of labor in the fields, most women to a life of grinding, chopping, and cooking. "Servitude," said my mother as she prepared home-cooked breakfast, dinner, and tea for eight to ten people three hundred and sixty-five days a year. She was right. Churning butter and skinning and cleaning hares, without the option of picking up the phone for a pizza if something goes wrong, is unremitting, unforgiving toil. Perhaps, though, my mother did not realize how much worse her lot might have been. She could at least buy our bread from the bakery. In Mexico, at the same time, women without servants could expect to spend five hours a day—one-third of their waking hours—kneeling at the grindstone preparing the dough for the family's tortillas. Not until the 1950s did the invention of the tortilla machine release them from the drudgery. . . .

In the 1880s, the industrialization of food got under way long after the production of other common items of consumption, such as textiles and clothing, had been mechanized. Farmers brought new land into production, utilized reapers and later tractors and combines, spread more fertilizer, and by the 1930s began growing hybrid maize. Steamships and trains brought fresh and canned meats, fruits, vegetables, and milk to the growing towns. Instead of starving, the poor of the industrialized world survived and thrived. . . .

To us, the cheap jam, the margarine, and the starchy diet look pathetic. Yet white bread did not cause the "weakness, indigestion, or nausea" that coarse whole wheat bread did when it supplied most of the calories (not a problem for us since we never consume it in such quantities). Besides, it was easier to detect stretchers such as sawdust in white bread. Margarine and jam made the bread more attractive and easier to swallow. Sugar tasted good, and hot tea in an unheated house in mid-winter provided good cheer. For those for whom fruit had been available, if at all, only from June to October, canned pineapple and a Christmas orange were treats to be relished. For the diners, therefore, the meals were a dream come true, a first step away from a coarse, monotonous diet and the constant threat of hunger, even starvation.

Nor should we think it was only the British, not famed for their cuisine, who were delighted with industrialized foods. Everyone was, whether American, Asian, African, or European. . . .

For all, Culinary Modernism had provided what was wanted: food that was processed, preservable, industrial, novel, and fast, the food of the elite at a price everyone could afford. Where modern food became available, populations grew taller and stronger, had fewer diseases, and lived longer. Men had choices other than hard agricultural labor, women other than kneeling at the *metate* [stone grinding tool] five hours a day.

Culinary Luddism Is Elitist

So the sunlit past of the Culinary Luddites never existed. So their ethos is based not on history but on a fairy tale. So what? Perhaps we now need this culinary philosophy. Certainly no one would deny that an industrialized food supply has its own problems, problems we hear about every day. Perhaps we *should* eat more fresh, natural, local, artisanal, slow food. Why not create a historical myth to further that end? The past is over and gone. Does it matter if the history is not quite right?

It matters quite a bit, I believe. If we do not understand that most people had no choice but to devote their lives to growing and cooking food, we are incapable of comprehending that the foods of Culinary Modernism—egalitarian, available more or less equally to all, without demanding the disproportionate amount of the resources of time or money that traditional foodstuffs did—allow us unparalleled choices not just of diet but of what to do with our lives. If we urge the

Mexican to stay at her *metate*, the farmer to stay at his olive press, the housewife to stay at her stove instead of going to McDonald's, all so that we may eat handmade tortillas, traditionally pressed olive oil, and home-cooked meals, we are assuming the mantle of the aristocrats of old. We are reducing the options of others as we attempt to impose our elite culinary preferences on the rest of the population.

If we fail to understand how scant and monotonous most traditional diets were, we can misunderstand the "ethnic foods" we encounter in cookbooks, at restaurants, or on our travels.... We can represent the peoples of the Mediterranean, Southeast Asia, India, or Mexico as pawns at the mercy of multinational corporations bent on selling trashy modern products—failing to appreciate that, like us, they enjoy a choice of goods in the market, foreign restaurants to eat at, and new recipes to try. A Mexican friend, suffering from one too many foreign visitors who chided her because she offered Italian, not Mexican, food, complained, "Why can't we eat spaghetti, too?"

A Culinary Ethos That Opens Food Choices for Everyone

If we unthinkingly assume that good food maps neatly onto old or slow or homemade food (even though we've all had lousy traditional cooking), we miss the fact that lots of industrial foodstuffs are better. Certainly no one with a grindstone will ever produce chocolate as suave as that produced by conching in a machine for seventy-two hours. Nor is the housewife likely to turn out fine soy sauce or miso. And let us not forget that the current popularity of Italian food owes much to the availability and long shelf life of two convenience foods that even purists love, high-quality factory pasta and canned tomatoes. Far from fleeing them, we should be clamoring for more high-quality industrial foods....

Culinary Luddites are right, though, about two important things. We need to know how to prepare good food, and we need a culinary ethos. As far as good food goes, they've done us all a service by teaching us how to use the bounty delivered to us (ironically) by the global economy. Their culinary ethos, though, is another matter. Were we able to turn back the clock, as they urge, most of us would be toiling all day in the fields or the kitchen; many of us would be starving. Nostalgia is not what we need. What we need is an ethos that comes to terms with contemporary, industrialized food, not one that dismisses it, an ethos that opens choices for everyone, not one that closes them for many so that a few may enjoy their labor, and an ethos that does not prejudge, but decides case by case when natural is preferable to processed, fresh to preserved, old to new, slow to fast, artisanal to industrial. Such an ethos, and not a timorous Luddism, is what will impel us to create the matchless modern cuisines appropriate to our time.

"*Conventionally grown whole foods also often have lower levels of antioxidants and other beneficial phytochemicals than the same foods grown organically.*"

Organic Foods Are Healthier than Non-Organic Foods

Deborah Rich

While the designation of foods produced without the use of agrichemicals as organic began in the 1950s, only recently has consumer interest in purchasing organic foods increased. As more and more companies market products to these consumers, some have begun to wonder about the advantages of eating these foods. In the viewpoint that follows, Deborah Rich argues that one of the major benefits of organic foods is their increased nutrient content. Rich cites multiple studies showing that organically grown foods contain higher levels of important nutrients than conventionally grown foods. The low nutritional content of conventionally grown foods that most Americans consume, Rich suggests, has resulted in grave consequences for the nation, including higher rates of chronic disease, nutrient deficiencies, and

Deborah Rich, "Not All Apples Are Created Equal," *Earth Island Journal*, vol. 23, no. 1, Spring 2008. Copyright © 2008 by Earth Island Institute. All rights reserved. Reproduced by permission.

overeating. Deborah Rich is a journalist who has written about agriculture for the San Francisco Chronicle, OnEarth *magazine, and the* Washington Post.

As you read, consider the following questions:

1. In the study by Donald R. Davis cited by Rich, what nutrients declined in conventionally grown foods as compared with organic?

2. What are some of the chronic diseases that could be combated by nutrients present in high levels in organic foods, according to studies by Lukas Rist and the University of California, Davis?

3. As stated by the author, why does less-nutrient-dense food contribute to people's overeating?

D on't ask the US federal government whether there are any health benefits to eating organic food. It won't tell. No mere coincidence, then, that no pictures of farmers or farms (or fertilizers or pesticides) appear in the USDA [United States Department of Agriculture] food pyramid logo. The federal government encourages the consumption of more fruits, vegetables, and grains, but stops short of evaluating the farming systems that produce these same foods. An apple is an apple regardless of how it has been grown, the USDA food pyramid suggests, and the only take-home message is that we should all be eating more apples and less added sugars and fats.

But this message may be too simplistic. Over the past decade, scientists have begun conducting sophisticated comparisons of foods grown in organic and conventional farming systems. They're finding that not all apples (or tomatoes, kiwis, or milk) are equal, especially when it comes to nutrient and pesticide levels. How farmers grow their crops affects, sometimes dramatically, not only how nutritious food is, but also how safe it is to eat. It may well be that a federal food policy that fails to acknowledge the connection between what happens on the farm and the healthfulness of foods is enough to make a nation sick.

Farming Practices Impact Nutrient Content

In the late 1990s, researcher Anne-Marie Mayer looked at data gathered by the British government from the 1930s to the 1980s on the mineral contents of 20 raw fruits and vegetables. She found that levels of calcium, magnesium, copper, and sodium in vegetables, and of magnesium, iron, copper, and potassium in fruit had dropped significantly.

The 50-year period of Mayer's study coincides with the post–World War II escalation of synthetic nitrogen and pesticide use on farms. These agrichemicals allowed farmers to bypass the methods of maintaining soil fertility by replenishing soil organic matter with cover crops, manure, and compost, and of controlling pests with crop rotation and intercropping. Reliance on chemical fertilizers and pesticides became a defining characteristic of conventional farming, while farmers who eschewed the use of agrichemicals came to be considered organic.

In 2004, Donald R. Davis, a research associate with the Biochemical Institute at the University of Texas at Austin, published a similar analysis of data collected by the USDA in 1950 and again in 1999 on the levels of 13 nutrients in more than 40 food crops. Davis found that while seven nutrients showed no significant changes, protein declined by six percent; phosphorous, iron, and calcium declined between nine percent and 16 percent; ascorbic acid (a precursor of vitamin C) declined 15 percent; and riboflavin declined 38 percent. Breeding for characteristics like yield, rapid growth, and storage life at the expense of taste and quality were likely contributing to the decline, Davis hypothesized. The "dilution effect," whereby fertilization practices cause harvest weight and dry matter to increase more rapidly than nutrient accumulation can occur, probably also played a role, Davis suggested.

Meanwhile, researchers at the Rodale Institute in Pennsylvania were seeing a trade-off between use of synthetic fertilizers and food nutrient values in the institute's Farming Systems Trial.

"We looked at the major and minor nutrients of oat leaves and seeds, grown after 22 years of differentiation under conventional and organic systems," says Paul Hepperly, research and training manager at the institute. "We found a direct correlation between the increase of organic matter and the amount of individual minerals in the oat leaves and seeds. The increase in minerals ranged from about seven percent for potassium, up to 74 percent for boron. On average, it was between 20 and 25 percent for all the elements we looked at, and we looked at nitrogen, phosphorous, potassium, calcium, magnesium, sulfur, iron, manganese, copper, boron, and zinc. The production practices used on these oats were completely the same the year they were planted—the plots varied only by the legacy of what had happened to the soil as a result of the previous farming practices. This showed how dramatic the soil change had been and its effect on the nutrient content of the plant. We've done these tests not only on oats but also on wheat, corn, soybeans, tomatoes, peppers, and carrots, and we consistently find that the organic heritage improves soil and improves the mineral content of the food products."

Probably due in part to a fertilizer effect, and partly because the use of chemical pesticides dampens the mobilization of a plant's own defenses, conventionally grown whole foods also often have lower levels of antioxidants and other beneficial phytochemicals than the same foods grown organically.

Charles Benbrook, chief scientist at the Organic Center and former executive director of the Board on Agriculture [and Natural Resources] of the National Academy of Sciences, maintains a database of all the studies published since 1980 that compare the nutrient levels of organic and conventional foods. His analysis of food comparison studies shows that, on average, conventionally grown fruits and vegetables have 30 percent fewer antioxidants than their organically grown counterparts. This makes enough of a difference, says Benbrook, that "consumption of organic produce will increase average daily antioxidant intake by about as much as an additional serving of most fruits and vegetables."

Organic Farming Could Reduce Incidence of Chronic Disease

The public health implications of farming methods that restore food nutrient density are tantalizing. Several studies released in 2007 suggest that moving US agriculture toward organic practices could help to reduce the incidence of some of our nation's most debilitating and costly chronic diseases.

At the University of California at Davis, researchers compared organic and conventional tomatoes: They found that 10-year mean levels of quercetin were 79 percent higher in organic tomatoes than in conventional tomatoes, and levels of kaempferol were 97 percent higher. Quercetin and kaempferol are flavonoids, which epidemiological studies suggest offer protection from cardiovascular disease, cancer, and other age-related diseases.

A study led by Lukas Rist, head of research at the Paracelsus hospital in Switzerland, demonstrated how farm practices affect health even several levels up the food chain. Rist analyzed milk samples from 312 breast-feeding mothers. He found that mothers consuming at least 90 percent of their dairy and meat from organic sources have 36 percent higher levels of rumenic acid in their breast milk than mothers eating conventional dairy and meat. Rumenic acid is one of a group of compounds that nutritional research suggests have anti-carcinogenic, anti-diabetic, and immune-modulating effects, and that favorably influence body fat composition.

Photosynthesis on Steroids

Plants that receive ample to excessive water and nutrients, especially nitrogen, receive what amounts to a big physiological jolt, leading to what one scientist called "photosynthesis on steroids." This . . . increases the production of chloroplasts within plant cells, which increase the photosynthetic production of sugars, the precursors of carotenoids. . . .

This is why beta-carotene and vitamin A are often higher in conventional fruits and vegetables—the carotenoids . . . make use of extra energy and nutrients. These same conditions, however, are what markedly increase the nitrate levels in fruits and vegetates, which is not desirable for overall plant or human health. . . .

In most high-yield, conventional farming systems where nitrogen is supplied in excess, plants grow vigorously with an abundance of vegetative growth . . . , produce extra chloroplasts, and hence elevated levels of carotenoids, but delay the reproductive process and production of vitamin C. Such plants also experience a buildup of nitrates (a negative for food safety and nutritional quality). . . .

Conversely, in organic systems, levels of vitamin C are typically elevated compared to plants grown in high-nitrogen systems, and there is little build up of nitrates, while beta-carotene levels are also somewhat depressed. This allows these plants to better deal with stresses from pests and climatic extremes, because of their enhanced ability to scavenge free radicals via vitamin C and other antioxidant systems.

*Charles Benbrook et al., "New Evidence
Confirms the Nutritional Superiority of Plant-Based
Organic Foods,"* The Organic Center State of Science Review:
Nutritional Superiority of Organic Foods, *March 2008.*

Nutrition Deficiencies Result from Low-Nutrient-Dense Foods

Eager as we are to connect the dots between specific nutrients and specific health benefits, we're still a long way from being able to understand or predict the effect of raising or lowering nutrient levels in one food or another. As Michael Pollan writes in his new book *In Defense of Food*, "Even the simplest food is a hopelessly complicated thing to analyze, a virtual wilderness of chemical compounds, many of which exist in intricate and dynamic relation to one another, and all of which together are in the process of changing from one state to another."

Long-term human feeding trials are notoriously difficult to control, and, though epidemiological studies show a correlation between eating fruits and vegetables and decreased incidence of disease, these studies don't identify which compounds in the food correspond with which health effects.

But even granting the many gaps in our knowledge of nutrient and health interactions, reducing the nutrient density of our whole foods seems a poor public health gamble. Americans already have trouble consuming the recommended daily amounts of fruits, vegetables, and whole grains. Diminishing the nutrient levels in the servings we do eat would seem to only compound our dietary problems.

Doctors don't see many patients walk into their clinics with obvious deficiency-related illnesses like scurvy, says Dr. Alan Greene, attending physician at Stanford University's Lucile Packard Children's Hospital. But doctors are, he says, seeing a lot of suboptimal intake of nutrients. "For instance, a huge percentage of the population doesn't get its recommended levels of calcium. Pregnant adult women should be getting 1,000 milligrams of calcium. By the time a healthy baby is born, the baby will have about 30,000 milligrams of calcium in its body, and all of that has to come from mom's diet or mom's body. The average mom is only getting about

700 milligrams a day during pregnancy, so that gap is mostly coming out of her bones, and is related to the osteoporosis we're seeing later."

Greene encourages patients to include fresh produce in their diets and to eat organic as much as possible. "I'll talk about how fruits and vegetables are really important, and that when you choose organic you're getting more of the great stuff, less of the bad stuff."

Overeating Is Caused by Foods with Less Nutrients

Unfortunately (or fortunately for those of us who like to eat), we haven't yet been able to design nutrient supplements that provide the same benefits as eating whole foods. "In all well-designed dietary intervention trials, where a carefully monitored amount of nutrients—vitamin C, vitamin E, antioxidants, etc.—were delivered to the animals or people in the form of fresh whole foods versus the same levels in the form of supplements, the animals or people who ate the whole foods universally responded better and were healthier," says Benbrook of the Organic Center.

Ironically, less-nutrient-dense foods may be partly why we're eating more and more. Phytochemicals contribute to the satisfaction we derive from foods. Some contribute to foods' flavor profiles, while others, like resveratrol, help trigger satiety. It could even be that the second helping is an instinctive attempt to secure sufficient micronutrients.

"In cattle and animals, this is known as hay belly," says Hepperly at the Rodale Institute. "If your hay gets rained on, you wind up with very low-quality hay because the water leaches out all the nutrients. You'll see animals eating more of this hay than they normally would. They get these big bellies, and they're unhealthy, but they're just trying to get their nutrients. Ranchers know that if they have animals with hay belly, they have poor-quality food. What we've done with the erosion of nutrient content in our foods—what we've done with additives, processing, and artificial production methods—is that we have basically produced a hay belly nation." . . .

The US Government Continues to Defer Judgment on Organic Foods

Try to get guidance from the federal government on the potential health benefits of eating organic, and you'll find your questions quickly and politely deflected. The US Department of Health and Human Services will defer to its Food and Drug Administration (FDA). FDA spokespeople will say that "organic" is a term used by the USDA, not the FDA, and that the FDA has no policy on organics. The USDA will say that its mandate does not extend to passing judgment on the relative safety and nutritional benefits of organic versus conventional foods, and that the USDA's task is simply to regulate use of the "certified organic" label.

With that passing of the apple, the federal government excuses itself from exploring whether conventional farming practices compromise the nutritional benefits of whole foods, and whether modern organic farming offers a model of food production that conveys significant health benefits. It's anyone's guess how many more studies will be needed before the relative merits of foods produced in different farming systems can become a topic of discussion among federal food and health officials. Agrichemical companies led by Monsanto will certainly use their considerable influence to delay that day as long as possible.

In the meantime, we will keep eating—but we need to ask just how well?

> *"What is clear from our analysis . . . is that there is currently no evidence of major differences in nutritional content between production regimens and from a public health perspective."*

Organic Foods Are Not Healthier than Non-Organic Foods

Alan D. Dangour, Elizabeth Allen, Karen Lock, and Ricardo Uauy

Following the introduction of organic production methods, many scientific studies have attempted to determine whether there is a difference in the nutritional quality of foods produced by these methods as compared with conventional methods. Over the years, many claims have been made touting the superiority of organics. However, in the viewpoint that follows, Alan D. Dangour, Elizabeth Allen, Karen Lock, and Ricardo Uauy dispute this view, arguing that they have found no evidence in the literature to support such a conclusion. The authors maintain that in their systematic review of only the best quality scientific studies con-

Alan D. Dangour, Elizabeth Allen, Karen Lock, and Ricardo Uauy, "Nutritional Composition & Health Benefits of Organic Foods—Using Systematic Reviews to Question the Available Evidence," *Indian Journal of Medical Research*, vol. 131, no. 4, April 2010, pp. 478–480. Copyright © Indian Council of Medical Research. All rights reserved. Reproduced by permission.

cerning the nutritional content of foods in relation to production methods, they found no significant nutritional differences between organically and conventionally produced foods. While they do identify some differences in nutrient content, they maintain that these variances would not make any impact on a person who is already consuming a healthy diet. Alan D. Dangour, Elizabeth Allen, and Karen Lock are lecturers, and Ricardo Uauy is a professor at the London School of Hygiene & Tropical Medicine.

As you read, consider the following questions:

1. As stated by the authors, with which standards and conditions must an organic farmer comply when producing foods?

2. What were some of the problems the authors encountered when reviewing the existing literature concerning the nutritional content of organic versus conventionally produced foods?

3. To what factor do the authors attribute the public criticism of their study?

Natural products vary in their nutritional composition both in their raw and processed states. At a qualitative level, this variability partly underlies the differences in sensory properties of food such as taste, texture and smell. However, at a quantitative level, the inherent variability also adds considerable complexity to research on the nutrient composition of foods. Fruit and vegetable crops vary in their nutritional composition depending on numerous factors such as the growing conditions and season, the fertiliser regime and the methods used for crop protection (*e.g.*, use of pesticides and herbicides). Animal source food products also vary in their nutritional composition depending on factors including the age and breed of the animal, the feeding regime and the season of production. The variability in the nutrient content of the raw food as produced, is then further increased during its storage, transportation and processing prior to consumption.

Determining the Influence of Agricultural Practices on Nutritional Content

It is intriguing to question whether certain agricultural practices can influence the nutritional composition of foodstuffs to such an extent that their impacts outweigh the combined influence of the numerous other factors important in defining nutritional composition. Indeed, there are several biologically plausible examples of significant impacts of agricultural production practices on the nutrient composition of foodstuffs. For example, the degree of protection from pests afforded to crops by farmers may influence the synthesis by plants of phytochemicals, such as phenolic compounds and flavonoids, which form part of the plant's inbuilt pest protection system. And similarly, the feeds provided to monogastric animals may alter the type and quantity of fats present in meat; for example, the nutritional quality of pork fat can be improved by feeding pigs with meals high in polyunsaturated fatty acids.

Organic farming, is an agricultural production method that has in recent years gained increasing prominence. There has been uncertainty over whether this method produces foodstuffs that are nutritionally distinct from those produced using conventional farming methods. Certified organic farmers produce foods according to a strict set of specified standards, which control the use of chemicals in crop production and medicines in animal production, and are required to pay particular attention to the impact of their farming practices on the wider environment. Organic standards differ between countries, many of which have their own organic certifying bodies, although some regional regulations do exist.

The Importance of Systematic Reviews

Recently published non-systematic reviews comparing nutrient composition of organically and conventionally produced foods have come to contrasting conclusions. Some have reported that organically produced foodstuffs have higher nutrient content than conventionally produced foodstuffs, while others have concluded that there are no consistent differences in nutrient content between production methods. However, all previous reviews comparing the nutrient content of organic and conventionally produced foods have been incomplete and non-systematic, and very few have undertaken new statistical analysis of existing published data.

The importance of systematic reviews to bring together and critically evaluate all available evidence has long been recognized, and systematic reviews are used internationally to define public health policy. In contrast to non-systematic reviews, which can be biased and incomplete, the prime purpose of systematic reviews of literature is to provide a comprehensive display of all available evidence in a common format. Systematic reviews have clearly defined guidelines for their conduct. The review process starts with the preparation of a protocol, which among other things explicitly states the research question, the search terms and inclusion/exclusion criteria, and the requirements for defining quality in studies. The review protocol must be peer reviewed and made available for public scrutiny, and this pre-specification of review methods helps ensure unbiased selection of relevant papers and abstraction of relevant data. The advantages of the systematic approach are clear—reviews are comprehensive, and bias is minimized. Only by systematically reviewing all of the available evidence can a comprehensive and impartial conclusion be drawn, which can be used by policy makers and consumers alike to make informed decisions.

The UK [United Kingdom] Food Standards Agency, an independent Government department set up by an Act of Parliament in 2000 to protect the public's health, and consumer interests, in relation to food, has been under increasing pressure from various groups to make a statement on the nutritional quality of organic foods, and in late 2007 requested that a systematic review be conducted on this topic. Our team at the London School of Hygiene & Tropical Medicine tendered for, and was awarded, a contract from the UK Food Standards Agency to conduct a systematic review on the nutrient content of organic food, and our results were published in mid-2009.

Shortcomings in Existing Studies on Nutrition Content

On receipt of the contract, our first act was to constitute an independent expert panel to oversee, and advise on, the process of the review. We then wrote a review protocol which was peer reviewed and made publically available for comment. All relevant articles published with an abstract in English in a peer-reviewed journal since January 1958 (more than 50 yr) were identified. In reality, this involved screening more than 52,000 journal articles before identifying 162 that were relevant to our review question. We then checked the identified publications against our pre-specified quality criteria to determine whether their quality could be classified as satisfactory.

Our quality criteria were defined as the minimum we considered acceptable for scientific publications in this area: a clear definition of what was meant by "organic farming" with relation to the samples being tested; a statement of the cultivar of plant or breed of livestock under investigation; a statement of which nutrients were tested; specification of the laboratory methods used; and finally, identification of the methods used for statistical analysis. An alarming number of studies could not be classified as satisfactory quality; the most common omission was lack of information of the organic farming certifying body under which the foodstuffs were produced. Many studies also failed to state clearly exactly which crop cultivar or animal breed was assessed for nutrient content. In total, only 55 studies (34% of those identified) met our pre-specified quality criteria.

Notions of Organic Foods' Superiority Stoke Public Fears

There is currently no evidence to support or refute claims that organic food is safer and thus, healthier, than conventional food, or vice versa. Assertions of such kind are inappropriate and not justified, and remain groundless not only due to ethical considerations but also because of limited scientific data. The selective and partial presentation of evidence serves no useful purpose and does not promote public health. Rather, it raises fears about unsafe food. The lack of trust in agricultural and industrial methods of production and in food quality gives rise to nagging feelings of uncertainty and insecurity; consumers are left in confusion and ignorance, counting the widely publicized food scares. Available research . . . does not support nor refute consumer perceptions regarding the superiority of organic food. Unfortunately, knowledge of the differences between organic and conventional produce is extremely limited with respect to the more potent food safety hazards, like microbial pathogens and mycotoxins. Still, for many years now, consumers perceive organic food as having certain intrinsic safety and quality characteristics. Many supporters of organic farming believe that an agricultural system is more than the sum of its parts, and rely on personal experiences and beliefs that make them more receptive to the idea that organic food is indeed superior.

Faidon Magkos, Fotini Arvaniti, and Antonis Zampelas,
"Organic Food: Buying More Safety or Just Peace of Mind?
A Critical Review of the Literature," Critical Reviews in
Food Science and Nutrition, *January/February 2006.*

Statistical analysis was hampered by shortcomings in the data presented in published studies. Formal meta-analysis was not feasible as many studies failed to present information on sample size or variability in nutrient content, and analysis by individual foods was also not possible because of a lack of sufficient data on specific foods. Instead, we conducted analysis by nutrient group (*e.g.*, vitamin C or phenolic compounds) and, in order to avoid multiple statistical testing which can result in spurious findings, we restricted our analysis to those 11 nutrient groups that had been reported in 10 or more studies.

No Evidence of Differing Nutritional Content

The results of our statistical analysis of data extracted from satisfactory quality studies found no evidence of differences between organically and conventionally produced crops for 8 of the nutrient groups analysed including vitamin C, phenolic compounds, magnesium and zinc. We did, however, identify some statistically significant differences between production regimen which are also biologically plausible. First, we identified that conventionally produced foods contain more nitrogen, probably because of the greater use of nitrogen fertilisers in conventional than in organic farming methods. Secondly we showed that organic crops contained more phosphate, which may relate to differences in nutrient content of soil between production regimens. Production regimen and particularly differences in fertiliser use and soil management are likely to impact on nutritional composition of crops. What is clear from our analysis, however, is that there is currently no evidence of major differences in nutritional content between production regimens and from a public health perspective, the differences that we did identify are not important in the context of a normal healthy diet.

In a second review, using a similar fully peer-reviewed systematic process, we sought to determine if there was any evidence of nutrition-related health benefits from consumption of organic foods. Despite an extensive search process which identified more than 92,000 papers, we only found 11 relevant publications that were of extremely variable quality. Our conclusion from this second review is that there is currently no evidence of any nutrition-related health benefits from consuming organic foods.

The Conflict of Scientific Evidence and Personal Beliefs

It would be fair to say that our reviews have received a mixed response and it might prove instructive to examine the reasons for this a little more closely. While many members of the public and the scientific community thanked us for providing much-needed clarity on the question of nutrient content, some people felt that differences between production regimen in the chemical residue content of foods was a more important question. We agree that this latter question is indeed important and would probably warrant further systematic review, but it is wrong to criticise our work for not including this topic. We stated very clearly at the outset that we were reviewing only the evidence on nutritional composition and nutrition-related health benefits, which are important questions for the agricultural industry, public health nutritionists and consumers. What is also clear from the numerous responses we have received is that there is a widely held belief that in contrast to organic farming, conventional farming practices produce poor-quality foods and cause widespread environmental degradation. We make no comment at all about environmental factors in our review, as these concerns were beyond the scope of our work, but it would seem that provision of robust scientific evidence that questions personal beliefs is not always welcomed.

Systematic reviews are comprehensive and impartial and should be used to answer important policy-relevant questions.

Based on the existing evidence, our reviews have drawn into question previous claims of nutritional superiority and nutrition-related health benefits of organic foods, although we have also highlighted the generally poor quality of the evidence base. We urge agricultural scientists working in this area to improve the quality of their research, possibly by collaborating with public health nutritionists and epidemiologists, and hope that we have provided policy makers and consumers with useful evidence to help them make informed choices.

| "While hunger anywhere on the planet is horrid and preventable, having it in America is truly unforgivable."

Hunger Is Still a Problem in America

Joel Berg

While publicity has raised global awareness about global hunger, relatively few people know about the food insecurity problems that continue to plague millions of Americans. In the viewpoint that follows, Joel Berg highlights this problem, arguing that in a nation as developed and wealthy as the United States, no person should go hungry. While Berg concedes that very few Americans die as a direct result of malnutrition today, he laments the incidence of individuals living in the United States who have insufficient access to food to consume a healthy diet. He cites low wages, insufficient government funds allotted to food assistance programs, increasing food costs, and inequality of wealth as causes of hunger, and he argues that all are forecast to worsen in coming years. Berg, though, remains hopeful that hunger can be eradicated in the United States as more and more people become aware of the plight facing their fellow citizens. Joel Berg is a

Joel Berg, *All You Can Eat: How Hungry Is America?* New York: Seven Stories Press, 2008, pp. 13–18. Copyright © 2008 by Seven Stories Press. All rights reserved. Reproduced by permission.

longtime food and hunger activist and the executive director of the New York City Coalition Against Hunger.

As you read, consider the following questions:

1. As stated by Berg, on average, how much did workers earning minimum wage make in a year, and how much did they pay out in rent (when the federal minimum wage was $5.15)?

2. According to Berg, what was the most recent decade when children in America were still dying of hunger?

3. By how much have food costs been rising in recent years, according to the US Department of Agriculture statistics cited by Berg?

Try explaining to an African that there is hunger in America. I've tried, and it's not easy.

In 1990, while on vacation, I was wandering alone through the dusty streets of Bamako, the small capital of the West African nation of Mali, when a young man started walking alongside me and struck up a conversation. At first, I thought he wanted to sell me something or ask me for money, but it turned out he just wanted to talk, improve his English, and learn a little about America. (He had quickly determined by my skin color that I was non-African and by my sneakers that I was American.)

When he asked me whether it was true that everyone in America was rich, I knew I was in trouble. How could I explain to him that a country as wealthy as mine still has tens of millions suffering from poverty and hunger? How could I explain to him that America—the nation of Bill Gates, "streets paved with gold," Shaquille O'Neal, and all-you-can-eat buffets—actually has a serious hunger problem? That—in a country without drought or famine and with enough food and money to feed the world twice over—one in eight of our own people struggles to put food on their tables? . . .

Hunger in America Is Unforgivable

I tried to tell him that not all Americans were as rich as he thought, and that much of the wealth he saw was concentrated among a small number of people while the majority toiled to make a basic living. I explained that living in a cash economy such as America's presents a different set of challenges than living in a subsistence and barter-based economy that exists in much of Mali. That in America, you have to pay a company for oil, gas, and all other basic necessities. You must pay a landlord large sums of money to live virtually anywhere. That while many workers in America earn a minimum wage equaling less than $11,000 a year for full-time work (the US federal minimum wage was then $5.15 per hour), they often pay more than $1,500 per month in rent, which equals $18,000 per year. So, many actually pay *more* in rent than they earn. Then they have to figure out a way to pay for health care, child care, transportation, and yes, food. When Americans have expenses that are greater than their income, they must go without basic necessities.

I thought I was very persuasive, but I still don't think I ultimately convinced him. Given that English was likely his third or fourth language, perhaps he didn't precisely understand what I was saying. Perhaps concepts such as paying for child care didn't resonate with him since few Malians pay others to care for their children. Moreover, I bet that—all my caveats aside—$11,000 a year sounded like a great deal of money to him.

Standing there in Africa, for the first time in my life I briefly had a hard time convincing even myself that hunger in the US was something that I should seriously worry about given that things were obviously so much worse elsewhere. After all, I was forced to consider that, as bad as hunger is in America, US children rarely starve to death anymore, while they still do in parts of the developing world.

But then I recalled all the people I had met throughout America who couldn't afford to feed their families—who had to ration food for their children, choose between food and rent, or go without medicine to be able to buy dinner—and I reminded myself that, just because they weren't quite dropping dead in the streets, that didn't mean that their suffering wasn't significant indeed. And then I further reminded myself that America *was* the nation of Bill Gates—and more than 400 other billionaires, not to mention more than 7 million millionaires—so it was particularly egregious that my homeland allowed millions of children to suffer from stunted growth due to poor nutrition. I thus came back to the same conclusion I reach every day: While hunger anywhere on the planet is horrid and preventable, having it in America is truly unforgivable. . . .

A Phenomenon as American as Apple Pie

When people look at the facts for themselves, they discover the shocking reality: Hunger amidst a sea of plenty is a phenomenon as American as baseball, jazz, and apple pie. Today in the United States—because tens of millions of people live below the meager federal poverty line and because tens of millions of others hover just above it—35.5 million Americans, including 12.6 million children, live in a condition described by the federal government as "food insecurity," which means their households either suffer from hunger or struggle at the brink of hunger.

Primarily because federal antihunger safety net programs have worked, American children are no longer dying in significant numbers as an immediate result of famine-like conditions—though children did die of malnutrition here as recently as the late 1960s. Still, despite living in a nation with so many luxury homes that the term "McMansion" has come into popular usage, millions of American adults and children have such little ability to afford food that they do go hungry

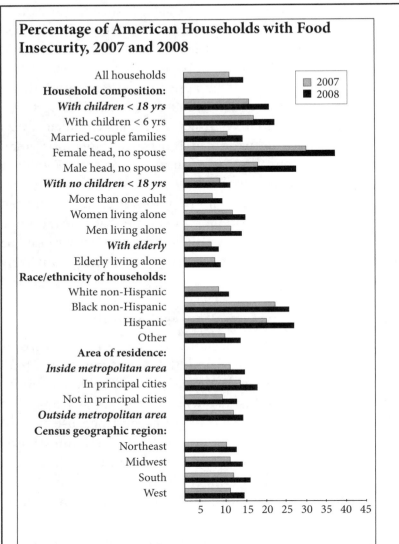

Percentage of American Households with Food Insecurity, 2007 and 2008

All households
Household composition:
With children < 18 yrs
With children < 6 yrs
Married-couple families
Female head, no spouse
Male head, no spouse
With no children < 18 yrs
More than one adult
Women living alone
Men living alone
With elderly
Elderly living alone
Race/ethnicity of households:
White non-Hispanic
Black non-Hispanic
Hispanic
Other
Area of residence:
Inside metropolitan area
In principal cities
Not in principal cities
Outside metropolitan area
Census geographic region:
Northeast
Midwest
South
West

2007
2008

5 10 15 20 25 30 35 40 45

NOTE: *Food insecurity* is defined by the USDA as "a household-level economic and social condition of limited or uncertain access to adequate food."

TAKEN FROM: Economic Research Service and U.S. Department of Agriculture, 2007 and 2008.

at different points throughout the year—and are otherwise forced to spend money on food that should have been spent on other necessities, like heat, health care, or proper child care.

Most alarmingly, the problem has only gotten worse in recent years. The 35.5 million food-insecure Americans encompass a number roughly equal to the population of California. That figure represents a more than 4-million-person increase since 1999. The number of children who lived in such households also increased during that time, rising by more than half a million children. The number of adults and children who suffered from the most severe lack of food—what the [George W.] Bush administration now calls "very low food security" and what used to be called "hunger"—also increased in that period from 7.7 million to 11.1 million people—a 44 percent increase in just seven years.

While once confined to our poor inner cities (such as Watts, Harlem, Southeast DC, the Chicago South Side, and the Lower Ninth Ward of New Orleans) and isolated rural areas (such as Appalachia, the Mississippi delta, Indian reservations, and the Texas/Mexico border region), hunger—and the poverty that causes it—has now spread so broadly it is a significant and increasing problem in suburbs throughout the nation.

More Americans Are Dependent on Food Pantries

Meanwhile, just as more people need more food from pantries and kitchens, these charities have less to give. Since the government and private funding that they receive is usually fixed, when food prices increase, charities are forced to buy less. When those fixed amounts from government actually decrease (as they have in recent years), the situation goes from worse to worser.

In May 2008, America's Second Harvest Food Bank network—the nation's dominant food bank network (which, in late 2008, changed its name to Feeding America)—reported that 100 percent of their member agencies served more clients [than] in the previous year, with the overall increases estimated to be between 15 to 20 percent. Fully 84 percent of food banks were unable to meet the growing demand due to a combination of three factors: increasing number of clients; decreasing government aid; and soaring food prices.

The number of "emergency feeding programs" in America—consisting mostly of food pantries (which generally provide free bags of canned and boxed groceries for people to take home) and soup kitchens (which usually provide hot, prepared food for people to eat on-site)—has soared past 40,000. As of 2005, a minimum of 24 million Americans depended on food from such agencies. Yet, given that more than 35 million Americans were food insecure, this statistic meant that about 11 million—roughly a third of those without enough food—didn't receive any help from charities.

Inequality and Increasing Food Costs

We live in a new gilded age. Inequality of wealth is spiraling to record heights and the wealthiest are routinely paying as much as $1,500 for a case of champagne—equal to five weeks of full-time work for someone earning the minimum wage. While welfare reform is still moving some families to economic self-sufficiency, families being kicked off the rolls are increasingly ending up on the street. Homelessness is spiking. Poverty is skyrocketing. And the middle class is disappearing.

Meanwhile, soaring food prices made it even more difficult for families to manage. Food costs rose 4 percent in 2007, compared with an average 2.5 percent annual rise for the 1990–2006 time period, according to the US Department of Agriculture (USDA). For key staples, the hikes were even worse: milk prices rose by 7 percent in 2007 and egg costs rose by a whopping 29 percent.

It was even tougher for folks who wanted to eat nutritiously. A study in the Seattle area found that the most nutritious types of foods (fresh vegetables, whole grains, fish, and lean meats) experienced a 20 percent price hike, compared to 5 percent for food in general. The USDA predicted that 2008 would be even worse still, with an overall food price rise that could reach 5 percent, and with prices for cereal and bakery products projected to increase as much as 8.5 percent. . . .

Awareness of the Hunger Problem Is Rising

From 1970 to 2005, the mass media ignored hunger. But due to the surge of intense (albeit brief) media coverage of poverty in the aftermath of Hurricane Katrina, and subsequent reporting of food bank food shortages and the impact of increasing food prices on the poor, the American public has been slowly waking to the fact that hunger and poverty are serious, growing problems domestically. Plus, more and more Americans directly suffer from hunger, have friends or relatives struggling with the problem, or volunteer at feeding charities where they see the problem for themselves.

Harmful myths about poverty are also starting to be discredited. While Americans have often envisioned people in poverty as lazy, healthy adults who just don't want to work, 72 percent of the nation's able-bodied adults living in poverty reported to the Census Bureau in 2006 that they had at least one job, and 88 percent of the households on food stamps contained either a child, an elderly person, or a disabled person. It is harder and harder to make the case that the trouble is laziness and irresponsibility. The real trouble is the inability for many working people to afford to support their families on meager salaries, and the inability of others to find steady, full-time work.

> "Our global goal should be that all people enjoy food security: reliable access to a sufficient quantity, quality, and diversity of food to sustain an active and healthy life."

Hunger Is Still a Problem Around the World

Ismail Serageldin

Throughout the final years of the twentieth century, international organizations banded together to fight the global problem of hunger. The efforts of these organizations in coordination with individuals and national governments helped to alleviate the problem. However, as Ismail Serageldin argues in the following viewpoint, many people still remain without secure food sources. The author identifies the main obstacles to food security, and he offers solutions to some of the most pressing issues—limited land and water, climate change, and the use of aquatic resources— focusing on the need to employ science and technology as a tool for creating stable food supplies. Ismail Serageldin formerly served as the chairman of the Consultative Group on International Agricultural Research and is currently the director of Egypt's Library of Alexandria.

Ismail Serageldin, "Abolishing Hunger," *Issues in Science & Technology*, vol. 25, no. 4, Summer 2009, pp. 35–38; Fall 2009 by the University of Texas at Dallas, Richardson, TX. Reprinted with permission.

As you read, consider the following questions:

1. As stated by the author, how many people were hungry around the world in 2008?

2. In what areas does the author believe progress must be made to achieve global food security?

3. What type of technological developments in plants does the author encourage to combat the global hunger problem?

The first of the Millennium Development Goals, which were adopted by the world's leaders at the United Nations in 2000, was a promise to fight poverty and reduce the number of the hungry by half by 2015, from 850 million to 425 million hungry souls on this planet. Shame on us all! By 2008, the figure had actually risen to 950 million and is estimated to reach 1 billion in a few years.

Hunger Is the New Global Shame

It is inconceivable that there should be close to a billion people going hungry in a world as productive and interconnected as ours. In the 19th century, some people looked at slavery and said that it was monstrous and unconscionable; that it must be abolished. They were known as the abolitionists, and they were motivated not by economic self-interest but by moral outrage.

Today the condition of hunger in a world of plenty is equally monstrous and unconscionable, and it too must be abolished. We must become the new abolitionists. We must, with the same zeal and moral outrage, attack the complacency that would turn a blind eye to this silent holocaust, which causes some 40,000 hunger-related deaths every day.

As we celebrate the bicentennial of Abraham Lincoln, the founder of the U.S. National Academy of Sciences and the Great Emancipator, it behooves us to become these new abolitionists. Lincoln said that a house divided cannot stand and that a nation cannot survive half free and half slave. Today, I say a world divided cannot stand; humanity cannot continue living partly rich and mostly poor.

Our global goal should be that all people enjoy food security: reliable access to a sufficient quantity, quality, and diversity of food to sustain an active and healthy life. Most developed countries have achieved this goal through enormous advances in agricultural techniques, plant breeding, and engineering schemes for irrigation and drainage, and these advances are making a difference in developing countries as well. The Malthusian nightmare [an idea based on the work of British political economist Thomas Malthus] of famine checking population growth has been avoided. Global population has grown relentlessly, but many lagging societies have achieved a modicum of security that would have been unthinkable half a century ago. India, which could not feed 450 million people in 1960, is now able to provide the food energy for a billion people, plus a surplus, with essentially the same quantities of land and water.

Steps Must Be Taken to Increase Food Security

Still, much more needs to be done. Achieving global food security will require progress in the following areas:

- Increasing production to expand the caloric output of food and feed at rates that will match or exceed the quantity and quality requirements of a growing population whose diets are changing because of rising incomes. This increase must be fast enough for prices to drop (increasing the accessibility of the available food to the world's poor) and be achieved by increasing the productivity of the small farmers in the less-developed countries so as to raise their incomes even as prices drop.

- Such productivity increases will require all available technology, including the use of biotechnology, an approach that every scientific body has deemed to be safe but is being bitterly fought by the organic food growers' lobby and various (mainly European) nongovernmental organizations.

- Climate change has increased the vulnerability of poor farmers in rain-fed areas and the populations who depend on them. Special attention must be given to the production of more drought-resistant, saline-resistant, and less-thirsty plants for the production of food and feed staples.

- Additional research is needed to develop techniques to decrease post-harvest losses, increase storability and transportability, and increase the nutritional content of popular foods through biofortification.

- Biofuels should not be allowed to compete for the same land and water that produce food for humans and feed for their livestock. We simply cannot burn the food of the poor to drive the cars of the rich. We need to develop a new generation of biofuels, using cellulosic grasses in rain-fed marginal lands, algae in the sea, or other renewable sources that do not divert food and feed products for fuel production.

- Because it is impractical to seek food self-sufficiency for every country, we need to maintain a fair international trading system that allows access to food and provides some damping of sudden spikes in the prices of internationally traded food and feed crops.

- The scientific, medical, and academic communities must lead a public education campaign about food security and sound eating habits. Just as we have a global antismoking campaign, we need a global healthy food initiative.

- And we need to convince governments to maintain buffer stocks and make available enough food for humanitarian assistance, which will inevitably continue to be needed in various hot spots around the world.

No single action is going to help us solve all the problems of world hunger. But several paths are open to us to achieve noticeable change within a five-year horizon. Many policy actions are already well understood and require only the will to pursue them. But there are a few more actions that will become effective only when combined with the development of new technologies that are almost within our grasp. Critical advances in the areas of land, water, plants, and aquatic resources will enable us to take a variety of actions that can help put us back on track to significantly reduce hunger in a few short years.

Land Must Be Conserved and Utilized Properly

Agriculture is the largest claimant of land from nature. Humans have slashed and burned millions of hectares of forest to clear land for farming. Sadly, because of poor stewardship, much of our farmland is losing topsoil, and prime lands are being degraded. Pressure is mounting to further expand agricultural acreage, which means further loss of biodiversity due to loss of habitat. We must resist such pressure and try to protect the tropical rain forests in Latin America, Africa, and Asia. This set of problems also calls for scientists to:

- Rapidly deploy systematic efforts to collect and classify all types of plant species and use DNA fingerprinting for taxonomic classification. Add these to the global seed/gene banks and find ways to store and share these resources.

- Use satellite imagery to classify soils and monitor soil conditions (including moisture) and launch early warning campaigns where needed.

- For the longer term, conduct more research to understand the organic nature of soil fertility, not just its chemical fertilizer needs.

New Strategies for Water Use Must Be Developed

Water is life. Humans may need to consume a few liters of water per day for their survival and maybe another 50 to 100 liters for their well-being, but they consume on average about 2,700 liters per day for the food they consume: approximately one liter per calorie, and more for those whose diet is rich in animal proteins, especially red meat. At present, it takes about 1,200 tons of water to produce a ton of wheat, and 2,000 to 5,000 tons of water to produce a ton of rice. Rainfall is also likely to become more erratic in the tropical and subtropical zones where the vast majority of poor humanity lives. Floods alternating with droughts will devastate some of the poorest farmers, who do not have the wherewithal to withstand a bad season. We absolutely must produce "more crop per drop." Some of what needs to be done can be accomplished with simple techniques such as land leveling and better management of irrigation and drainage, but we will also need plants that are better suited to the climate conditions we expect to see in the future. Much can be done with existing knowledge and techniques, but we will be even more successful if we make progress in four critical research areas:

- First, we know hardly anything about groundwater. New technologies can now map groundwater reservoirs with satellite imagery. It is imperative that an international mapping of locations and extent of water aquifers be undertaken. New analysis of groundwater potential is badly needed, as it is likely that as much as 10% of the world's grain is grown with water withdrawals that exceed the recharge rate of the underground reservoirs on which they draw.

- Second, the effects of climate change are likely to be problematic, but global models are of little help to guide local action. Thus, it is necessary to develop regional modeling for local action. Scientists agree on the need for these models to complement the global models and to assist in the design of proper water strategies at the regional and local scales, where projects are ultimately designed.

- Third, we need to recycle and reuse water, especially for peri-urban agriculture that produces high-value fruits and vegetables. New technologies to reduce the cost of recycling must be moved rapidly from lab to market. Decision makers can encourage accelerated private-sector development programs with promises of buy-back at reliable prices.

- Finally, the desalination of seawater, not in quantities capable of supporting all current agriculture, but adequate to support urban domestic and industrial use, as well as hydroponics and peri-urban agriculture, is possible and important.

New Plants Must Be Researched and Engineered

Climate change is predicted to reduce yields unless we engineer plants specifically for the upcoming challenges. We will need a major transformation of existing plants to be more resistant to heat, salinity, and drought and to reach maturity during shorter growing seasons. Research can also improve the nutritional qualities of food crops, as was done to increase the vitamin A content of rice. More high-risk research also deserves support. For example, exploring the biochemical pathways in the mangrove that enable it to thrive in salty water could open the possibility of adding this capability to other plants.

Too much research has focused on the study of individual crops and the development of large monoculture facilities, and this has led to practices with significant environmental and social costs. Research support should be redirected to a massive push for plants that thrive in the tropics and subtropical areas and the arid and semiarid zones. We need to focus on the farming systems that are suited to the complex ecological systems of small farmers in poor countries.

This kind of research should be treated as an international public good, supported with public funding and with the results made freely available to the poor. Such an investment will reduce the need for humanitarian assistance later on.

Marine Resources Should Be Farmed

In almost every aspect of food production, we are farmers, except in aquatic resources, where we are still hunter-gatherers. In the 19th century, hunters almost wiped out the buffaloes from the Great Plains of the United States. Today, we have overfished all the marine fisheries in the world, as we focused our efforts on developing ever more efficient and destructive hunting techniques. We now deploy huge factory ships that can stay at sea for months at a time, reducing some species to commercial extinction.

We need to invest in the nascent technologies of fish farming. There is some effort being made to promote the farming of tilapia, sometimes called the aquatic chicken. In addition, integrating some aquaculture into the standard cropping techniques of small farmers has proven to be ecologically and economically viable. The private sector has invested in some high-value products such as salmon and shrimp. But aquaculture is still in its infancy compared to other areas of food production. A massive international program is called for.

Marine organisms reproduce very quickly and in very large numbers, but the scientific farming of marine resources is almost nonexistent. Proper farming systems can be devised that will be able to provide cheap and healthy proteins for a growing population. About half the global population lives near the sea. Given the billions that have gone into subsidizing commercial fishing fleets, it is inconceivable that no priority has been given to this kind of highly promising research. Decision makers must address that need today.

Science and Technology Will End Hunger

Science has been able to eke out of the green plants a system of food production that is capable of supporting the planet's human population. It is not beyond the ken of scientists to ensure that the bounty of that production system is translated into food for the most needy and most vulnerable of the human family.

Science, technology, and innovation have produced an endless string of advances that have benefited humanity. It is time that we turn that ingenuity and creativity to address the severe ecological challenges ahead and to ensure that all people have that most basic of human rights, the right to food security.

Most of the necessary scientific knowledge already exists, and many of the technologies are on the verge of becoming deployable. It is possible to transform how we produce and distribute the bounty of this earth. It is possible to use our resources in a sustainable fashion. It is possible to abolish hunger in our lifetime, and we need to do so for our common humanity.

Periodical Bibliography

The following articles have been selected to supplement the diverse views presented in this chapter.

Sharon Begley — "Feeding the 900 Million: Let Them Eat Micronutrients," *Newsweek*, September 20, 2008.

Artemis Dona and Ioannis S. Arvanitoyannis — "Health Risks of Genetically Modified Foods," *Critical Reviews in Food Science & Nutrition*, February 2009.

David Katz — "The Case for Natural Foods," *Prevention*, March 2010.

Frederick Kaufman — "The Second Green Revolution," *Popular Science*, February 2011.

Bonnie Liebman — "In Your Face: How the Food Industry Drives Us to Eat," *Nutrition Action Healthletter*, May 2010.

Conrad Miller — "Today's Synthetic Foods: Shrinking Our Brains, Testicles, and Livers?" *Tikkun*, September–October 2009.

Mehmet Oz — "The Organic Alternative," *Time*, August 18, 2010.

Debra Van Camp et al. — "The Paradox of Organic Ingredients," *Food Technology*, November 2010.

Neil Zevnik — "The Organic Conundrum, or What About Local?" *Better Nutrition*, September 2009.

OPPOSING
VIEWPOINTS®
SERIES

CHAPTER 2

What Should Be Done to Improve Nutrition and Fight Obesity?

Chapter Preface

In April 2010 the board of supervisors in Santa Clara, California, enacted legislation to ban the inclusion of toys with children's meals at fast-food restaurants, unless the food served met nutrition guidelines set by the board. On April 28 Supervisor Ken Yeager was quoted in the *Los Angeles Times* as saying, "This ordinance breaks the link between unhealthy food and prizes." Yeager and others on the board argued that fast-food chains were using the lure of free toys to entice children into adopting bad eating habits. Other concerned health experts nationwide have asserted that even exposing children to foods with poor nutrition is a temptation that may encourage unwise food choices. For this reason, several school boards throughout the United States have voted to remove nonnutritious foods from school cafeterias and vending machines on campus.

For advocates of such policies, the health benefits seem certain especially because high obesity rates among children suggest that young people are eating too many high-calorie foods and not getting enough exercise. Margo Wootan, director of nutrition policy at the Center for Science in the Public Interest, states on the organization's website, "We need programs and policies that make healthy food more available, that disclose the calorie content of restaurant foods, and that teach people how to make healthy eating easier." Because nearly one-third of children in America are overweight, President Barack Obama authorized his administration to achieve the outcomes that Wootan and others promote. The president created the Task Force on Childhood Obesity in February 2010 to help spread nutrition information, increase availability of nutritious food in schools to underprivileged children, and assist parents in making better food choices.

Kelly D. Brownell, a Yale psychologist at the Rudd Center for Food Policy and Obesity, supports this more active role of government in public nutrition. In a May 11, 2010, opinion piece for journalist Mark Bittman's website, Brownell contends that "scaling back industry practices that contribute to ill health, creating better food and activity conditions, and doing so in ways that support parents, protect vulnerable populations, and make it easier for people to lead healthier lives seems a reasonable and responsible role for government to play." Critics, however, are not convinced that government should dictate personal eating habits. In response to the Santa Clara ban on toys with children's fast-food meals, a spokesperson for McDonald's USA argued in a statement released to the Consumer Ally website, "The proposal does not reflect what consumers want, nor is it something they asked for. Parents tell us it's their right and responsibility—not the government's—to make their own decisions and to choose what's right for their children." These challengers maintain that removing toys from children's meals does not teach nutrition, and it may herald government intrusion into other potential causes of childhood obesity such as too much time spent in front of computers, televisions, and video games.

In the following chapter, various authors debate whether government should become involved in regulating nutrition in the United States and whether mandated policies can effectively fight obesity. While some believe that dictating personal choice will foster a bloated and meddling "nanny state," others insist that the health of the nation and its ability to compete in the future demand policies that encourage citizens to be physically well and fit.

> *"Some motivated consumers will use information on the label or menu to guide their food choices."*

Mandatory Nutrition Labeling Will Help People Make Healthful Food Choices

Joanne E. Arsenault

In the following viewpoint, Joanne E. Arsenault argues the merits of nutrition labeling on store-bought and restaurant foods. According to Arsenault, food labeling has given consumers more knowledge about the foods they eat and motivated some people, as various studies report, to opt for healthier food choices. Though she acknowledges that research so far has not shown that nutrition labeling reduces obesity, she maintains that mandatory labeling is still positively impacting consumer behavior. Joanne E. Arsenault is a nutrition policy analyst in the Food, Nutrition, and Agricultural Policy Research program of RTI International, a health research institute.

As you read, consider the following questions:

1. As Arsenault reports, in what year was the Nutrition Labeling and Education Act (NLEA) implemented?

Joanne E. Arsenault, "Can Nutrition Labeling Affect Obesity?" *Choices: The Magazine of Food, Farm and Resource Issues*, 3rd Quarter 2010. Reproduced with permission.

2. According to a 1990 Health and Diet Survey cited by the author, what percentage of consumers reported changing their minds about buying a food product because they read the nutrition label?

3. As Arsenault writes, in the year the NLEA was enacted, the FDA estimated that food labeling could save the country how much in health care costs over the ensuing twenty years?

Current estimates of obesity in the United States indicate that 68% of adults and 32% of children are overweight or obese. The incidence of obesity has risen dramatically over the past two decades [since the 1990s]. Obesity in an individual is the result of an energy imbalance in intake and output, but the cause of this imbalance on a population level is not fully understood. Changes in the food environment, including the proliferation of convenience and fast foods high in energy and fat content, have paralleled the obesity epidemic. One approach to combating obesity is to educate the public about nutrition and the nutritional components of the food they purchase. Nutrition labeling of foods sold in stores and in restaurants, when available, is designed to provide the public with information to make informed choices about food purchases. The presumption for an obesity impact is that knowledge about the calorie content of foods will motivate and/or guide individuals to consume the appropriate amount of calories for proper weight management.

Food Labeling Legislation in the United States

The Nutrition Labeling and Education Act (NLEA) of 1990, implemented in 1994, provided the U.S. Food and Drug Administration (FDA) with the authority to require nutrition labeling on packaged foods and require that certain nutrient-related claims be consistent with agency regulations. The objectives of the NLEA were to clear up confusion about label information, help consumers make healthful food choices, and encourage manufacturers to produce healthier food products. Specific nutrients were required to be listed, including calories, calories from fat, saturated fat, and sugars; and the nutrient information per serving had to be placed in the context of a daily diet. In 2003, regulation for labeling of trans fat was added.

An FDA Obesity Working Group was formed in 2003 and directed by the FDA commissioner to improve the food label and thereby assist consumers in preventing weight gain and reducing obesity. The group recommended giving calories more prominence on the food label. FDA is currently looking into "front-of-package" nutrition labeling that consists of brief nutrient-specific information such as calorie content in a serving or a summary symbol representing overall quality. The intent is that front-of-package labeling is simpler and easier to understand than the Nutrition Facts Panel on the side or back of the product.

The NLEA only applies to packaged foods sold in stores, but food consumed away from home, such as in restaurants, has increased substantially during the past few decades, from 18% to 32% of total daily calorie intake. The new health care legislation, the Health Care and Education Reconciliation Act of 2010, mandates calorie labeling of foods sold in restaurant chains with more than 20 outlets and vending machines. The legislation pertains to calories, but contains a clause to include other nutrients, and stipulates that a statement must be posted regarding suggested daily caloric intake so consumers can put the information in the context of a daily diet. . . .

Impact of Food Labeling on Consumer Behavior

For food labeling to impact consumers' health and weight status, consumers must use the information. They must first read the label, understand the information and how to use it, and then make decisions about their food consumption based on the information. According to the 2008 Health and Diet Survey conducted by FDA, 54% of consumers reported often using the food label when purchasing a food item for the first time. There are indications of increased use of food label information in the years immediately after the implementation of NLEA. In the 1990 Health and Diet Survey, 30% of consumers said they changed their minds about buying a food product because they read the nutrition label. By the end of 1995, approximately one year after the food labeling legislation went into effect, 48% had done so. That figure has remained stable, with 49% of respondents in the 2008 survey reporting changing their minds about purchasing a product based on reading the nutrition label.

Information on nutrient content of foods alone does not necessarily affect dietary behavior. Food choices are influenced by many factors, and consumers must be motivated to use the information for their health. Awareness of diet and health relationships is an important motivational factor for dietary behavior. A USDA [U.S. Department of Agriculture] food intake survey conducted in the 1990s asked participants about both food intake and nutrition knowledge and found that those who were aware of health problems associated with saturated fat and cholesterol consumed less of those nutrients.

Some studies have shown that people who are aware of diet-disease relationships use food labels to guide their food choices, and that food label use is associated with better dietary intake choices. A [1999] survey in Washington State found that belief in the importance of a low-fat diet and knowledge of the association between diet and cancer strongly predicted food label use, and that food label use was significantly associated with lower fat intake. In a nationally representative survey conducted in 1994–1996, food label use was associated with higher overall dietary quality as measured by the USDA's Healthy Eating Index. More recently, individuals in the National Health and Nutrition Examination Survey (NHANES), 2005–2006, who had a chronic condition such as diabetes, hypertension, or hyperlipidemia reported reading food labels more than those without any of these conditions— 71% versus 60% for the sample. Among individuals with one or more of these conditions, those who read food labels consumed more fiber and less sugar than those who did not read labels. Another study using the same NHANES data set reported that overweight individuals were more likely to use food labels.

One objective of the NLEA was to encourage manufacturers to produce healthier food products. The NLEA allowed for nutrition content claims on products, such as "low-fat" or "reduced-fat," if the product met specific criteria. Considerable increases in the number and sales of fat-modified foods were documented within the year after the NLEA went into effect. However, these products are not necessarily lower in calories than similar foods with higher fat content because the fat is often replaced with sugar. Therefore, consumption of these products does not necessarily lead to lower overall energy intake.

Potential Impacts of Labeling on Health and Obesity

Impacts of nutrition labeling on health outcomes is more difficult to assess directly. When the NLEA was enacted, an FDA economic impact analysis estimated that the food label could save up to $26 billion in health care costs over the next 20 years based on estimated reductions in heart disease and cancer due to dietary improvements. Only one study to date has since estimated an impact of NLEA on obesity and health-associated cost savings. The study [conducted in 2006] examined data before and after NLEA from an annual national health survey, the National Health Interview Survey, which

"Foods that are bad for you. Foods that are really bad for you," by Russell T. Harris. www.CartoonStock.com.

asks about food label use and body weight. Body mass index (BMI) increased over the time period and label use remained steady. However, label users gained less BMI than nonusers, although the difference was only significant among non-Hispanic white females. It is unclear why the effect was only significant among that segment of the population. The study also estimated the potential economic impact of NLEA, based on estimated benefits from reduced BMI. The estimated value of benefits of NLEA among non-Hispanic white women was $166 billion over a 20-year period due to lower mortality risk, reduced medical expenditures, lower absenteeism, and increased productivity.

Some estimates of impacts on obesity have also been made with regard to nutrition labeling of restaurant menus. A recent [2010] study of pre and post calorie labeling of Starbucks' menu items estimated a 6% reduction in calories per sales transaction, and further projected a decrease in long-term body weight of less than 1%. An impact assessment in Los Angeles County [in 2009] estimated that restaurant menu labeling could decrease the annual weight gain of residents by 41%, based on estimates from other reports that 10% of restaurant patrons select reduced-calorie meals as a result of menu labeling with an average calorie reduction per meal of 100 kcal [kilocalorie].

Studies assessing the impact of nutrition labeling on obesity should be viewed with some caution. First, they are too few in number to make any definitive conclusions. Moreover, they are based on many assumptions often obtained from one study and extrapolated to a larger population. The optimal scientific study design would be a randomized trial where one group is exposed to nutrition labeling and a control group is not exposed, and both groups are followed over a long-term period to determine use of labeling, dietary intake, and body weight. Therefore, other factors affecting food intake and obesity would be evenly distributed among the two groups and differences in the outcomes could be attributed to labeling. It is likely that individuals with specific characteristics use labels to guide their daily food consumption, and these could be identified and accounted for in further extrapolations to predict impacts on a national population level. In reality, this type of study would not be feasible in a real-world setting; therefore, observational studies of label users and nonusers in various populations that control for other factors related to label use and health outcomes should be considered.

New options for labeling, such as front-of-package and restaurant menu item calorie information, should increase consumers' awareness of their calorie consumption. Menu labeling may result in reductions in fat and calorie content of menu items through recipe modification or reduction of portion sizes served. It is hard to imagine that a consumer would not be affected to some degree by knowledge that a selected entrée contains their entire recommended calorie intake for the day. However, the effect of menu labeling on consumers remains to be seen.

One could argue that the entire U.S. population has been exposed to nutrition labeling of foods for almost two decades and obesity is rising. Likewise, if obesity starts to decrease after mandatory menu labeling goes into effect, this does not infer causality. There are many other factors influencing obesity and a wide variety of efforts are being undertaken to tackle the obesity problem. Nevertheless, nutrition labeling of foods and menu items is important because consumers have a right to know what they are purchasing and consuming. Some motivated consumers will use information on the label or menu to guide their food choices. At the population level, nutrition labeling is just one of many efforts that will be needed to combat the obesity epidemic.

> "*Even those [study participants] who indicated that the calorie information influenced their food choices did not actually purchase fewer calories according to our data collection.*"

Mandatory Nutrition Labeling Will Not Necessarily Lead People to Make Healthful Food Choices

Brian Elbel, Rogan Kersh, Victoria L. Brescoll, and L. Beth Dixon

In the following viewpoint, Brian Elbel, Rogan Kersh, Victoria L. Brescoll, and L. Beth Dixon reveal the results of a study they conducted regarding the influence of calorie labeling upon consumer eating habits at fast-food restaurants. The authors targeted fast-food franchises in low-income areas in two New York City communities, because the health problems that pervade both low-income and racially diverse populations are often blamed on poor diet. After collecting data from a variety of these restaurants that either did or did not institute food labeling, the

Brian Elbel, Rogan Kersh, Victoria L. Brescoll, and L. Beth Dixon, "Calorie Labeling and Food Choices: A First Look at the Effects on Low-Income People in New York City," *Health Affairs*, vol. 28, no. 6, November–December 2009, pp. 1110–1121. Copyrighted and published by Project HOPE/HealthAffairs. The published article is archived and available online at www.healthaffairs.org.

group found no appreciable difference in the calorie intake of customers. That is, in the authors' findings, calorie labeling did not influence many customers to make better food choices at the restaurants under examination. Brian Elbel, Rogan Kersh, and L. Beth Dixon are professors at New York University, and Victoria L. Brescoll is a professor at Yale University.

As you read, consider the following questions:

1. According to the authors, how many states and cities in the United States have introduced menu nutrition labeling as of the writing of the viewpoint?

2. As the researchers report, how many calories did New York City customers purchase before menu labeling was instituted? How many calories did they purchase after labeling was instituted?

3. Why do the authors believe more research has to be done to validate or refute these findings?

Several years after the U.S. Surgeon General's public warning [in 2001] of an "obesity epidemic," public policy responses have been patchwork and partial. Although more than 100 bills have been introduced since 2002, no major legislation to address the problem has passed the U.S. Congress to date. States and metropolitan areas vary widely in the degree and nature of their legislative and regulatory activity. Experts in the science and politics of nutrition have reached some consensus around feasible policy options that could have an impact on rising obesity rates. However, few of these options have been implemented on a scale that would permit systematic evaluation.

Some Cities Try Calorie Labeling

One recently emergent and rapidly expanding policy to address obesity rates is calorie labeling (also referred to as menu labeling). New York City [NYC] became the first U.S. jurisdiction to implement this legislation, on 19 July 2008. Although the proposed regulatory details differ across localities, the statutes typically require restaurants with a certain number of locations in a city or state (ranging from at least five to twenty; the number in New York City is fifteen) to visibly post the caloric content of all regular menu items. In general, fast-food outlets must post calorie labels on their menu boards; sit-down establishments are required to list calories on the printed menu. In some cases, additional nutritional information is required. NYC restaurants must list calories for all regularly available menu options, using a typeface and format similar to the price or name of the item.

Nutrition advocates view labeling as an important public policy tool to influence obesity at a population level, largely because of the strong link between fast-food consumption and obesity. More than thirty U.S. cities and states, including the nation's most populous city (New York) and state (California), have introduced legislation to mandate menu labeling; thirteen bills had become law as of this writing. At the federal level, consensus around a labeling bill seems to have emerged in the Senate. This bill, which at the time of this writing has been rolled into the larger set of bills addressing health reform, is very similar to the NYC legislation.

Past Research and the Present Study

Little scientific evidence exists evaluating the influence of menu labeling on fast-food choices. One study by the NYC Department of Health and Mental Hygiene examined food purchases at Subway restaurants that voluntarily posted calorie information in advance of mandatory labeling. They found that Subway customers who saw the information (32 percent of respondents) consumed fifty-two fewer calories, on average. The study could not account for health-conscious consumers who might have been more likely to notice calorie information and therefore purchased fewer calories because of their underlying preferences. A recent experiment using random assignment of consumers in a non-restaurant setting found that menu labeling did not decrease calories ordered or consumed, even among those who reported noticing the calorie information. In fact, that study found some evidence that males ordered more calories when labels were present. A second experiment examining calorie labeling on a printed menu found that labeling was effective in altering food consumed, but only when coupled with information indicating that 2,000 was the recommended daily allowance of calories. Finally, a few studies have examined menu labeling in a cafeteria setting or via hypothetical-choice experiments. These studies found inconsistent and generally weak results from menu labeling.

Using data collected before and after labeling was introduced in New York City and a comparison location (Newark, New Jersey), we examined the influence of calorie labeling on food choices. Given the increased risk of obesity and related health problems associated with low-income and racially/ethnically diverse populations, we focused our attention on these groups. In addition to analyzing calories purchased at fast-food restaurants, we also examined the percentage of consumers who reported noticing and responding to calorie information.

Given the severe nature of this public health problem, careful scientific evaluations of policy solutions are incredibly important. There are many policy proposals ranging from educational interventions to attempts to change the built environment to make physical activity the "default" behavior in cities and states. However, almost none of these policy interventions has actually been implemented. Calorie-labeling policies are among the first obesity policies to be widely embraced. Yet we have virtually no data outside of the laboratory to examine whether these policies are effective and, in particular, whether they are effective among the most vulnerable populations. The study reported in this paper is the first to evaluate the effectiveness of this policy since its introduction.

Focusing on Lower-Income Neighborhoods

We chose New York City because it is the first site in the country to have introduced calorie labeling. We selected Newark as the control city because (1) it has not introduced calorie labeling; (2) its urban characteristics and demographics are similar to those of New York City; and (3) it does not have a vast number of daily commuters to New York City but is close enough to permit a reasonably consistent comparison.

We began by narrowing restaurants to those representing four of the largest fast-food chains located in New York City and Newark: McDonald's, Burger King, Wendy's, and KFC. We targeted restaurants within lower-income demographic areas that largely consist of minority groups, mostly African American and Latino. We used six sets of population-level characteristics to match two restaurants from the same chain in NYC neighborhoods with one restaurant of the same chain in the Newark city limits: population size, age, race/ethnicity, poverty level, obesity rates, and diabetes rates. We also attempted to match key structural or geographic characteristics in our restaurant pairings (for example, location relative to public transportation; proximity to large apartment complexes, hospitals, or other institutions; and location in a downtown area). After minimal restaurant substitutions, we were left with five restaurants in Newark and fourteen in New York (five Wendy's, eight McDonald's, three Burger King, and three KFC). In New York City, our data collection locations included four of the five boroughs: the Bronx (specifically, the South Bronx), Brooklyn (central Brooklyn), Manhattan (Harlem and Washington Heights), and Queens (the Rockaways).

All restaurants were visited during lunch (generally 12:30–3:00 p.m.) or dinner hours (generally 4:30–7:00 p.m.) for ap-

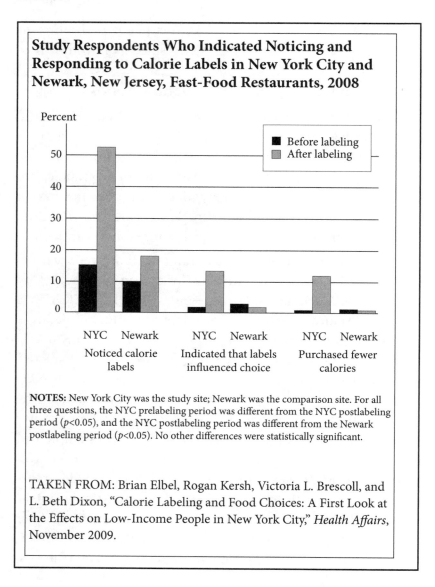

Study Respondents Who Indicated Noticing and Responding to Calorie Labels in New York City and Newark, New Jersey, Fast-Food Restaurants, 2008

Percent

Legend:
- Before labeling
- After labeling

NYC Newark
Noticed calorie labels

NYC Newark
Indicated that labels influenced choice

NYC Newark
Purchased fewer calories

NOTES: New York City was the study site; Newark was the comparison site. For all three questions, the NYC prelabeling period was different from the NYC postlabeling period ($p<0.05$), and the NYC postlabeling period was different from the Newark postlabeling period ($p<0.05$). No other differences were statistically significant.

TAKEN FROM: Brian Elbel, Rogan Kersh, Victoria L. Brescoll, and L. Beth Dixon, "Calorie Labeling and Food Choices: A First Look at the Effects on Low-Income People in New York City," *Health Affairs*, November 2009.

proximately 2.5 hours by a research team of three to four people. Restaurants were visited on a Tuesday, Wednesday, or Thursday (thereby avoiding days most likely to consist of "special" or "treat" meals) over a two-week period beginning 8 July 2008—before calorie labeling was implemented in New York City.

We used a methodology similar to a "street-intercept" survey. Every customer possible was approached as he or she entered the restaurant during our designated survey periods. Customers were asked to bring their receipts back and to answer a set of questions for compensation of $2. Subjects were not told why the receipts were being collected. It is difficult to assess cooperation rates with street-intercept surveys, and we did not directly collect participation data. However, another NYC study using the same method tracked the total number of customers entering a fast-food restaurant during data collection (regardless of whether customers were approached to take the survey) and found that 55 percent answered a survey. This was consistent with our data collection.

Approximately four weeks after labeling was introduced in New York City, data were again collected from the same restaurants, headed by the same research staff, using the same methodology, on the same days of the week and during the same time periods. To the extent that restaurants differ from each other in ways we cannot observe, these differences should be minimized by collecting data from the same locations both before and after labeling. Here we report on the results for respondents age eighteen and older. Because food choices that parents make for their children and that adolescents make for themselves are especially complex, we examined these groups in other work. We also limited our analysis to the food that adults purchased for their own consumption, given the difficulty in allocating calories from food items consumed by multiple people.

Collecting the Data

To gather valid nutrition data, study staff obtained receipts indicating food items purchased for each participant's own consumption. Food items purchased, along with any modifications or additions (for example, added cheese, regular or diet soda), were confirmed by study staff with oral review. We then used the nutrition data provided on each fast-food establishment's corporate Web site to manually calculate for each item purchased and for the order as a whole the following nutritional information: calories, saturated fat, sodium, and sugar. We chose these nutrients based on their associations with obesity, chronic disease, and overall health. All menu items and respective nutrition information were entered into a spreadsheet; all items were then verified by a second group of research assistants.

After the food purchase details were confirmed, a short survey was conducted that included respondent's age, sex, race (African American/black, Latino, other race/white), education (high school or less, some college or an associate degree, a bachelor's degree or above—these data were not collected at baseline), and whether the food was consumed in the restaurant or taken "to go." We also asked respondents (1) whether they noticed any calorie information posted in the establishment; (2) if so, whether the information influenced their food choices; and (3) whether this calorie information caused them to purchase more or fewer calories. . . .

After excluding twenty-one receipts for which specific food items could not be confirmed, we analyzed data from 1,156 receipts collected from adults for food they purchased for themselves. As per our design, 71 percent of our sample was surveyed in New York City (47 percent of these before calorie labeling and the rest after) with the remainder in Newark. Approximately 38 percent of our sample was male, with a mean age of thirty-eight. Those identifying themselves as black made up 65.7 percent of the sample; Latinos made up 19.9 percent; and the remaining 14.4 percent consisted of other races, including those identifying themselves as mixed race or white. Almost half of our post-labeling sample had only a high school diploma or less. Within cities, our sample stayed consistent, with the exception of a statistically significant increase in the proportion of black respondents in Newark (increasing from

74 percent pre-labeling to 81 percent post-labeling). Our New-ark sample was also slightly more likely to be black and less likely to be Hispanic than our NYC sample.

Those Who Reported Noticing Calorie Labels

At baseline, the percentage of people who saw calorie infor-mation available on posters, pamphlets, or food wrappers did not differ between New York City and Newark. However, after calorie labeling was instituted in New York City, the percent-age of respondents who reported noticing calorie information increased sharply in New York City—to 54 percent—but not in Newark.

New York City also saw an increase in the percentage of people who reported using this information and deciding as a result to purchase fewer calories. Newark saw no such in-creases. Put differently, 27.7 percent of our post-labeling NYC sample who saw the calorie labeling indicated that the infor-mation influenced their choices. Of these, approximately 88 percent indicated that they purchased fewer calories in re-sponse to labeling.

People in New York City purchased a mean number of 825 calories before menu labeling was introduced and 846 calories after labeling was introduced. The number of calories purchased in Newark before and after labeling also did not appreciably change (823 calories before labeling and 826 calo-ries after). Similar results were found for saturated fat, so-dium, and sugar, with no appreciable or significant differences before or after labeling was instituted.

[Another set of data] presents only the results for calories and whether these results differ by sex, race, or age. We found no evidence that any of these groups differed in their re-sponses to labeling, compared to the sample as a whole. In each case, we saw neither a difference between the NYC and Newark samples nor a difference before or after labeling.

We analyzed the number of calories purchased by (1) those who did not notice the posted calorie labels; (2) those who did notice the labels but indicated that they were not inclined to purchase fewer calories as a result; and (3) those who noticed the labels and indicated that as a result, they purchased fewer calories.

We first note that these relationships are not causal, given that seeing the labels (or not) could be correlated with other factors that induce people to purchase more or fewer calories. We found non-significant decreases in calories purchased for groups who indicated that the labels mattered to them (blacks and people under age thirty-five), while for other groups (older than age thirty-five) we found non-significant increases.

Results Show Little Variation

In our study of consumers from low-income, minority communities, calorie labeling increased the percentage of consumers who reported seeing calorie labels, and thereby the number of people who reported that the information influenced their food choices. This meaningful change as a result of labeling could "set the stage" for a larger influence of calorie labeling as time and public policy progress.

However, we did not find evidence in our sample that menu labeling influenced the total number of calories purchased at the population level. About half of the NYC respondents in our post-labeling sample reported noticing calorie information, and only a quarter of these reported that the information influenced their food choices. Even those who indicated that the calorie information influenced their food choices did not actually purchase fewer calories according to our data collection. We note again that our study sample consisted primarily of racial and ethnic minorities residing in relatively low-income areas; other groups may respond differently to labeling.

In an ideal world, calorie labeling on menus and menu boards would have an immediate and direct impact on everyone's food choices. However, as has been seen in previous attempts to change the behavior of vulnerable populations (for example, smoking cigarettes), greater attention to the root causes of behavior or multifaceted interventions, or both, will be necessary if obesity is to be greatly reduced in the overall U.S. population. Future policy development must consider this broader perspective.

> "Obesity has many causes, but some experts believe that the structure of [the Supplemental Nutrition Assistance Program] deserves some of the blame."

Food Stamp Programs Cause Obesity

Laura Vanderkam

In the viewpoint that follows, Laura Vanderkam acknowledges that obesity in America has many and diverse causes, but she indicts the food stamp program for encouraging binge buying of junk food among recipients. According to Vanderkam, the once-a-month disbursement of food stamps should be changed to bi-weekly disbursement to prompt recipients to ration their benefits and make better choices of purchased foods. In her opinion, giving out food stamps in one lump sum each month simply leads shoppers to spend all they have in one trip, prompting them to purchase more junk food and engage in "binge-starvation" cycles because they have the stamps and do not see the rationale of saving them for later trips during the month. Laura Vanderkam is a member of USA Today's *Board of Contributors and the author of* 168 Hours: You Have More Time than You Think.

Laura Vanderkam, "Do Food Stamps Feed Obesity?" *USA Today*, April 20, 2010.

As you read, consider the following questions:

1. As Vanderkam reports, how many Americans currently rely on food stamps to make food purchases?

2. According to Jay Zagorsky, why do food stamp recipients often fail to ration their benefits over each month?

3. As the author states, why do some advocates for the hungry object to the biweekly disbursement of food stamps?

Like kids in a cafeteria, Congress is busy these days complaining about school lunch. Reformers want to tighten nutrition standards because, as Kevin Concannon of the Agriculture Department told reporters recently [in April 2010], "Getting kids started eating healthier is one of the most important long-term goals we have as a country."

That's true, but school lunches already have to meet reasonable nutrition standards. The real next frontier in the war on obesity should be the Supplemental Nutrition Assistance Program (SNAP), or "food stamps." Some 38 million people—one in eight Americans—rely on this program, up from one in 50 in the 1970s. Food stamps have done a good job fighting hunger since their 1964 rollout, but as the program has grown, so has the percentage of Americans who are obese—from 13% in the early 1960s to about 35%. Now there's some evidence the two are related. Jay Zagorsky, a scientist at Ohio State University, has calculated that, controlling for socioeconomic status, women who received food stamps were more likely to be overweight than non-recipients. They gained weight faster while receiving assistance than when not.

The Habits of Food Stamp Users

Correlation is not causation, and obesity has many causes, but some experts believe that the structure of SNAP deserves some of the blame. As Americans debate how we can be healthier, the food stamp program deserves as critical a look as Congress is giving school lunch.

The one in eight Americans who rely on food stamps are a varied crew, from urban single moms to the "hipsters on food stamps" a recent [March 15, 2010] *Salon* article claimed to have discovered buying raw honey and shopping at organic markets. But for all the diversity, states run their programs pretty much the same way. Once a month, benefits are loaded electronically onto cards that can then be used at retailers.

This monthly cycle encourages certain habits. "A good chunk of people buy early in the month and store for later use," says Parke Wilde, a professor of nutrition at Tufts University who has studied shopping patterns and wrote a landmark 2000 paper on the topic. "The spending cycle is very, very sharp." In many cases, families spend most of their benefits in that first shop. They struggle to ration food evenly over a month (particularly since the average benefit is a not-so-princely $124 per person), and by week four, they are out of food and money.

One way or another, people make do, using food pantries, for instance. Wilde found that children's calorie consumption was even across the month. But women experienced a sharp calorie decline in week four for a simple reason: When times are tight, moms starve themselves so their kids can eat.

The result is that when the money comes through again, "you're literally shopping on an empty stomach," says Zagorsky. "We're not rational when food is in front of us." Anyone who has flipped through supermarket tabloids knows that this binge-dieting cycle packs pounds onto the celebrities who try it, before you even consider whether you're eating wholesome food or junk. Other women experience the same effect.

To be sure, not every SNAP recipient shops this way. Corbyn Hightower, a Sacramento-area mom of three who lost her job more than a year ago, says she shops two to three times a week at Trader Joe's, buying rice, beans and produce. Her car

Give Cash, Not Food Stamps

Food stamps work as intended, raising caloric consumption by as much as 10 percent more than if recipients were given cash. . . .

If we want the poor to consume less food, the remedy seems simple enough: Give them cash instead of food stamps—and let them make their own decisions about how much to consume. Experimental programs have demonstrated that "cashing out" food stamps is much more convenient for the poor and does not result in unhealthy diets nor the mismanagement of family finances. Recipients continued to get well above the recommended dietary allowances for most nutrients.

Douglas J. Besharov,
"Growing Overweight and Obesity in America:
The Potential Role of Federal Nutrition Programs,"
Testimony Before Senate Committee on
Agriculture, Nutrition and Forestry, April 3, 2003.

was a casualty of the recession, but on weekends she bikes to Whole Foods and carts home groceries in her bike trailer. She has also used food stamps to purchase seeds for a family garden, ensuring that she'll be able to harvest fresh produce daily this summer.

Though food stamp gardening is rare, Wilde found that people who shop frequently, like Hightower, don't experience the same deprivation cycle that could cause SNAP recipients to put on pounds. So Wilde and others have proposed a simple change: Pay SNAP money twice a month, not once.

Pilot Programs First

It's a neat answer. Unlike mailing actual "stamps," in this electronic era, the cost to do additional transfers is low, though there could be other problems. If people without cars don't live near supermarkets, it's inconvenient to take a cab twice a month or ask for rides. Some advocates for the hungry fear this would discourage participation. That's why a few states should try pilot programs and ask clients whether they like the new cycle before rolling it out broadly (initial reactions are, admittedly, mixed).

But it's important to note that even with twice-monthly transfers, families could still shop once a month if they wanted by saving up their benefits. It's just that the default behavior would be to shop more often. This makes switching the cycle a classic "nudge," a term popularized by behavioral economics experts Richard Thaler, a University of Chicago professor, and Cass Sunstein, the administrator of the White House Office of Information and Regulatory Affairs. You can do whatever you want, but the program provides a gentle push toward better choices.

Healthy choices are always a good idea, but now that President [Barack] Obama's health care reform bill is law, the American people have even more of a financial stake in questions of public health. You can argue whether programs such as food stamps should exist. If they do, though, they shouldn't make our medical woes worse. Reforming SNAP is an idea that deserves a look.

> "The weight of evidence from [various] studies indicates that for most program participants, food stamp benefits do not increase either body mass index ... or the likelihood of being obese."

Food Stamp Programs Do Not Cause Obesity

Michele Ver Ploeg and Katherine Ralston

Michele Ver Ploeg is an economist with the US Department of Agriculture Economic Research Service. Her work focuses on obesity and food assistance programs. Katherine Ralston is an agricultural economist with the same organization. In the viewpoint that follows, Ver Ploeg and Ralston examine recent studies analyzing the relationship between food stamps and obesity. According to the authors, these studies have offered no conclusive evidence of a link between the two. Ver Ploeg and Ralston also note that while some studies suggest a causal link among members of a certain demographic (such as women or teens), they maintain that creating policy to cater to these subgroups of food assistance recipients would be nearly impossible.

Michele Ver Ploeg and Katherine Ralston, "Food Stamps and Obesity: What We Know and What It Means," *Amber Waves*, vol. 6, no. 3, June 2008. Reproduced by permission.

As you read, consider the following questions:

1. How do Ver Ploeg and Ralston refute the notion that receiving food stamp benefits instead of cash can lead to overconsumption and, thus, weight gain?

2. As the authors explain, what is a selection bias and how does it apply to this research?

3. How long do most food stamp recipients receive benefits, according to Ver Ploeg and Ralston?

Critics of the food stamp program point to higher rates of obesity among some low-income populations and question whether the program might have been too successful in boosting food consumption. They assert that giving assistance in the form of benefits redeemable for food, instead of cash, has led participants to spend more on food and eat more than they would have otherwise. Others wonder if the monthly issuance of food stamp benefits is linked to boom-and-bust cycles of consumption that could lead to weight gain over the long term.

Reviewing the Research

A recent ERS [US Department of Agriculture Economic Research Service] report explores whether there is any evidence of a causal link between food stamp participation and obesity. ERS reviewed and synthesized the growing and sometimes conflicting research on the issue. Researchers placed greater weight on studies that used statistical methods to control for the fact that people choose to participate in the program and those who participate are likely to be different from those who do not in ways that researchers cannot always observe. These differences could be related to body weight.

The weight of evidence from these studies indicates that for most program participants, food stamp benefits do not increase either body mass index (BMI—a measure of weight adjusted for height) or the likelihood of being obese. A review of the research indicates that food stamp benefits do not increase the likelihood of being overweight or obese for men or children. For non-elderly adult women, who account for 28 percent of all food stamp participants, multiple studies show a potential link between food stamp receipt and an increase in obesity and BMI, although this effect appears to be small—about 3 pounds for a woman 5'4" to 5'6" tall. Some studies found that long-term participation in the program appears to heighten the impact on obesity.

It is not clear why participation in the food stamp program may increase the probability of obesity for women but not for men or children. Research about the causes underlying these results is not conclusive. Differences in energy requirements, activity levels, and eating patterns could be possible explanations. Because the food stamp program is administered as a household-level program, devising program changes that are appropriately targeted to household members who may be at risk of gaining weight, without harming those who are not and need the nutritional assistance, is a challenge. Policy changes that help program participants improve their overall diets or help them "smooth" their food consumption over periods of high and low income may be more effective. For example, issuing food stamp benefits on a biweekly, or even weekly basis, may help food stamp participants obtain and consume food on a more even basis.

Too Much Money for Food or Too Infrequently Issued?

The food stamp program is an entitlement program available to all U.S. households that meet the eligibility requirements pertaining to income, assets, work, and immigration status. Program benefits can be used to purchase almost any food sold by participating food retailers, except for food prepared in the store, hot foods, and alcohol and tobacco. The average monthly benefit level in 2007 was $96 per person and $215 per household, which translates roughly to $3.20 per person per day or $7.16 per household per day to spend on food. Most program participants spend some of their own money on food in addition to their monthly food stamp allotment.

There are two leading explanations for how food stamp benefits could contribute to weight gain that may lead to obesity. The first argues that restricting food stamp benefits to food purchases results in participants spending more money on food and, thus, consuming more food than they otherwise would if they did not participate in the program. Although food stamp benefits may have the intended effect of reducing undernourishment or underweight for at least some participants, this explanation implies that the benefits may also be pushing a portion of participants into overweight or obesity. If true, then one solution is to deliver food stamp benefits as cash. Cash benefits have been found to induce smaller increases in food spending than benefits that can be spent only on food.

But even if receiving food stamp benefits leads participants to spend more on food, it does not mean that the additional spending results in overconsumption and obesity. It is possible that food stamp benefits allow people to choose a different bundle of foods than they otherwise would. For example, participants may shift spending toward relatively more expensive foods that were previously out of reach (e.g., fresh meats versus canned beans or fresh fruit and vegetables instead of canned items). Or, since food stamps can be redeemed for food only in grocery stores, participation in the program may shift a household's food spending toward foods prepared and consumed at home, as opposed to food away from home. In either case, an increase in food expenditures would not necessarily lead to overconsumption of calories or a poorer diet.

The food stamp cycle explanation argues that the practice of distributing food stamps only once a month results in alternate periods of under- and overconsumption, a pattern dubbed the "food stamp cycle," which may result in weight gain. Households consume food every day but purchase food less regularly—every few days for some households, every few weeks for others. It is possible that food stamp participants run out of food (and benefits with which to purchase more food) near the end of the month. As food becomes scarce and food intake is restricted, a person may lose weight. Then, when food is abundant, the individual may overeat. This distorted pattern of consumption with its periods of binge eating gradually can lead to increased weight.

Teasing Out Cause and Effect

Two conditions can be associated with each other, without one being the cause and the other the effect. Food stamp benefits may be associated with increases in body weight but may not *cause* greater body weight if something else is to blame. Determining cause and effect is difficult because no experiments have been conducted comparing the body weights of participants randomly assigned to receive program benefits with those of others assigned to a comparison program (or lack of a program). Researchers must instead rely on nonexperimental methods that try to determine what would have happened if no one received food stamp benefits or if an alternative program to food stamps was implemented.

Comparing body weights of food stamp participants with those of eligible nonparticipants is an obvious starting point, but this approach may be problematic. Food stamp program participants may have different characteristics than those who are eligible for the program but choose not to participate. Very poor individuals, for example, may be more likely to participate than individuals who are less poor but still eligible. A household with a strong preference for food relative to other necessities may be more likely to apply for food stamps than an otherwise similar household. This strong preference for food may also lead to weight gain that would have occurred whether or not the household participated in the program.

While most studies try to control for as many differences between participants and nonparticipants as possible, it is likely that important differences are not observed. If these differences are related to body weight, then the estimated effects of food stamp participation could be biased. This bias is called selection bias because individuals self-select into the food stamp program. Researchers note that poverty is associated with higher risk of obesity in some population subgroups (for example, white women), but lower risk in others (among black and Hispanic men), suggesting that selection bias can be positive or negative in the case of food stamp participation and obesity. Accounting properly for selection bias can reveal a higher or lower risk of obesity than estimates that do not account for such bias.

ERS researchers reviewed over a dozen studies of the relationship between food stamp participation and BMI and the likelihood of obesity. Several of the earlier studies used cross-sectional data (observations of many individuals for a single point in time) and controlled for observed factors that might be related to body weight, such as age, race, sex, and education. While these studies are useful for understanding broad trends and highlighting possible relationships for further exploration, they do not account for potential selection bias and only observe individuals at a point in time, so they are of limited use in drawing causal conclusions.

The ERS review focused primarily on studies that attempt to control for selection bias (often using longitudinal data with multiple observations on the same individuals) and which are better able to tease out cause and effect between food stamp participation and weight. One can never be sure that these methods are truly picking up cause and effect, but the methods used in these studies help researchers get closer to that goal.

Diverse Effects Reflect Diverse Participants

The food stamp program serves a diverse population. In 2006, children accounted for almost half of all participants. Working-age women made up 28 percent of the caseloads, working-age men 13 percent, and the elderly age 60 and older 8 percent. Most of the food stamps issued go to households containing a child, elderly adult, or non-elderly disabled person (89 percent of all benefits). Many of the households receiving food stamps are single-adult households with children (34 percent). The ERS review of the effects of food stamp participation on body weight for this diverse group of participants found that food stamp participation has a small effect on obesity for adult women, but not for men or school-age children. Only a few studies have looked at children younger than 5 and the elderly, and they did not control for selection bias, so these subgroups are not discussed here.

Results for children ages 5–12 vary across sexes and differ in the direction of the relationship between food stamp participation and body weight. For young boys, studies found either no relationship between food stamp participation and BMI, or that food stamp participation is linked to a lower probability of being overweight (BMI-for-age greater than or equal to the 95th percentile).

For young girls, some studies found no association between food stamp participation and BMI. One study found that additional years of food stamp participation were associated with greater probability of being overweight. Another found a negative relationship between food stamp participation and being at risk of overweight (BMI-for-age greater than or equal to the 85th percentile). These two studies used different methodologies, which could account for the disparate results.

For adolescent children (ages 12–18), food stamp participation does not seem to be related to BMI or the probability of being overweight. None of the reviewed studies found a link between program participation and body weight for teenage boys or girls.

Only one reviewed study found a significant link between food stamp participation and BMI, overweight, or obesity status for men ages 19–59. That study found that food stamp participation by men was positively related to BMI but not to overweight or obesity. Previous studies comparing average BMI for men across food stamp participation and income levels found that for some racial and ethnic groups, food stamp participants had lower BMI than income-eligible nonparticipants and higher income men. In view of that, it is possible that either the positive effect of food stamps on BMI was not large enough to shift more men into the overweight (BMI greater than 25) and obese (BMI greater than 30) categories, or the shift in BMI was an improvement among underweight men.

Adult (ages 19–59) women are the only food stamp participants for which multiple studies show a link between food stamp participation and overweight. Not all studies showed that participation affects body weight. However, results from studies that used different techniques to control for selection bias indicate that food stamp participation may increase the probability that a woman is obese. The estimated 2- to 5-percentage-point change in the probability of being obese translates into a 5- to 21-percent increase in obesity rates. Other results show that food stamp participation is associated with an estimated 0.5-point increase in BMI for women, or about 3 pounds for a woman between 5'4" and 5'6" tall.

Over Longer Participation, Effects May Accumulate

The reviewed studies showed a stronger connection between long-term food stamp participation on body weight than short- or medium-term participation. Two studies found that women who received food stamp benefits for longer periods of time (one study defined "long term" as at least 2 consecutive years, the other as up to 5 consecutive years) increased the probability of being obese by 4.5 to 10 percentage points, which translates into a 20- to 50-percent increase in obesity rates.

Evidence is mixed with respect to long-term food stamp participation and men's weight. One study found no relationship between long-term participation (up to 5 consecutive years) on BMI or the probability of obesity for men. A second study found that participation for at least 2 consecutive years increased BMI and the probability of obesity for men, but shorter and repeated participation did not have these effects.

Most food stamp participants receive benefits for less than a year—the median length of food stamp participation is 6 to 8 months. Some participants, however, cycle on and off food stamps and others participate for longer periods. It is possible that small but positive effects of current food stamp participation on BMI may accumulate over longer, or shorter but repeated, periods and result in substantial total effects on BMI over time. Or, if the causal mechanisms underlying weight gain for women are related to periods of boom and bust surrounding the monthly issuance of food stamp benefits, then prolonged food stamp use could result in long-term weight gain. Further research may be able to tell a clearer story.

Implications for the Type and Timing of Benefits

One hypothesis of how food stamp participation causes weight gain is that benefit amounts are too high, causing participants to spend more money on food and, thus, consume more food than they otherwise would. One of the reviewed studies showed that the effect of food stamp participation on obesity is larger for single women than for women residing in households with more than one adult. Other research found that food stamps have little impact on the amount of money single women spend on food (i.e., the benefit amount is at least as big as what they otherwise would have spent on food). In that case, "cashing out" food stamp benefits to reduce overconsumption may not have the intended effect on body weight. The group whose weight is most affected by food stamp participation would not change their food spending if the benefits were shifted to cash.

Some studies measured participation as a dichotomous yes-or-no condition, while others looked at the amount of benefits the household received. Studies that used the amount of benefits to measure participation found a less consistent relationship between food stamp benefit levels and obesity as those that used the dichotomous measure. So, while some studies suggest a relationship between food stamp participation and obesity among women in particular, the research does not clearly indicate that higher benefit levels are associated with greater BMI and obesity, or that lower benefits would lead to lower BMI.

None of the studies reviewed explicitly tested whether boom-and-bust food consumption patterns associated with the benefit payment cycle contribute to obesity. If further studies find a causal link between the timing of benefits and disrupted patterns of consumption, possible policy solutions could include either increasing the frequency of benefit payments (biweekly or weekly) or raising the benefit amount, which could, paradoxically, help reduce obesity by reducing hungry days at the end of the benefit cycle.

The stronger relationship between food stamp participation and body weight found for women but not for men, the mixed relationships found for young boys and young girls, and the lack of any relationships found for adolescents make it difficult to come up with appropriate changes to the program to address obesity. Most food stamp benefits go to households that contain a child, elderly adult, or non-elderly disabled adult. Devising program changes that are appropriately targeted to household members who may be at risk of gaining weight, without harming those who are not, will be difficult. Nutrition education efforts and other programs that help improve the overall diets of all household members may be more effective.

> *"A consumer who drinks a conventional soft drink (20 oz [591 ml]) every day and switches to a beverage below this threshold would consume approximately 174 fewer calories each day."*

A Soda Tax Would Help Reduce Obesity

Kelly D. Brownell et al.

In the following viewpoint, Kelly D. Brownell and several colleagues argue that the consumption of sodas and other sugar-sweetened beverages may lead directly or indirectly to weight gain and other health problems. Because of the adverse effects associated with drinking these beverages, Brownell and his colleagues believe the government should impose an excise tax on caloric sweeteners that will raise the retail price of sugar-sweetened drinks. The authors contend that this tax will dissuade many people from drinking these beverages in excess and convince them to drink water or other healthier options. Kelly D. Brownell is a professor of psychology at Yale University. The co-authors of this viewpoint come from other academic institutions and various state health organizations.

Kelly D. Brownell et al., "The Public Health and Economic Benefits of Taxing Sugar-Sweetened Beverages," *New England Journal of Medicine*, vol. 361, no. 16, October 15, 2009. pp. 1599–1605. Copyright © 2009 by Massachusetts Medical Society. All rights reserved. Reproduced by permission.

As you read, consider the following questions:

1. In the two-year prospective study mentioned in this viewpoint, by what percentage did the risk for obesity increase for every sugar-sweetened beverage consumed per day by middle school students?

2. Why do the authors maintain that a sales tax or ad valorem excise tax on sugar-sweetened beverages would not serve the purpose of reducing the consumption of these drinks?

3. How do Brownell and his coauthors refute the objection that a soda tax would be regressive?

The consumption of sugar-sweetened beverages has been linked to risks for obesity, diabetes, and heart disease; therefore, a compelling case can be made for the need for reduced consumption of these beverages. Sugar-sweetened beverages are beverages that contain added, naturally derived caloric sweeteners such as sucrose (table sugar), high-fructose corn syrup, or fruit-juice concentrates, all of which have similar metabolic effects.

Taxation has been proposed as a means of reducing the intake of these beverages and thereby lowering health care costs, as well as a means of generating revenue that governments can use for health programs. Currently, 33 states have sales taxes on soft drinks (mean tax rate, 5.2%), but the taxes are too small to affect consumption and the revenues are not earmarked for programs related to health. This [viewpoint] examines trends in the consumption of sugar-sweetened beverages, evidence linking these beverages to adverse health outcomes, and approaches to designing a tax system that could promote good nutrition and help the nation recover health care costs associated with the consumption of sugar-sweetened beverages.

Consumption of Sugar-Sweetened Beverages Is Linked to Obesity

In recent decades, intake of sugar-sweetened beverages has increased around the globe; for example, intake in Mexico doubled between 1999 and 2006 across all age groups. Between 1977 and 2002, the per capita intake of caloric beverages doubled in the United States across all age groups. The most recent data (2005–2006) show that children and adults in the United States consume about 172 and 175 kcal [kilocalorie] daily, respectively, per capita from sugar-sweetened beverages.

The relationship between the consumption of sugar-sweetened beverages and body weight has been examined in many cross-sectional and longitudinal studies and has been summarized in systematic reviews. A meta-analysis showed positive associations between the intake of sugar-sweetened beverages and body weight—associations that were stronger in longitudinal studies than in cross-sectional studies and in studies that were not funded by the beverage industry than in those that were. A meta-analysis of studies involving children—a meta-analysis that was supported by the beverage industry—was interpreted as showing that there was no evidence of an association between consumption of sugar-sweetened beverages and body weight, but it erroneously gave large weight to several small negative studies; when a more realistic weighting was used, the meta-analysis summary supported a positive association. A prospective study involving middle school students over the course of 2 academic years showed that the risk of becoming obese increased by 60% for every additional serving of sugar-sweetened beverages per day. In an 8-year prospective study involving women, those who increased their consumption of sugar-sweetened beverages at year 4 and maintained this increase gained 8 kg [kilograms], whereas those who decreased their intake of sugar-sweetened beverages at year 4 and maintained this decrease gained only 2.8 kg.

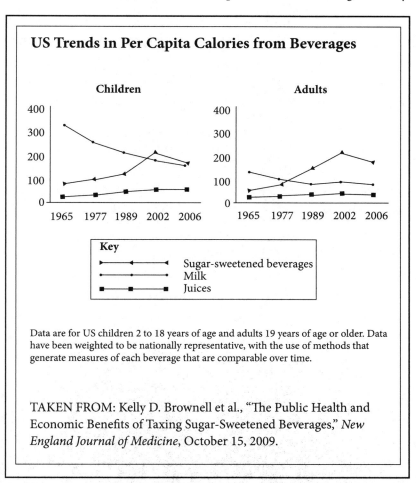

US Trends in Per Capita Calories from Beverages

Data are for US children 2 to 18 years of age and adults 19 years of age or older. Data have been weighted to be nationally representative, with the use of methods that generate measures of each beverage that are comparable over time.

TAKEN FROM: Kelly D. Brownell et al., "The Public Health and Economic Benefits of Taxing Sugar-Sweetened Beverages," *New England Journal of Medicine*, October 15, 2009.

Short-term clinical trials provide an experimental basis for understanding the way in which sugar-sweetened beverages may affect adiposity [obesity]. [In a 1990 study published in the *American Journal of Clinical Nutrition*, M.G.] Tordoff and [A.M.] Alleva found that as compared with total energy intake and weight during a 3-week period in which no beverages were provided, total energy intake and body weight increased when subjects were given 530 kcal of sugar-sweetened beverages per day for 3 weeks but decreased when subjects were given noncaloric sweetened beverages for the same length of time. [In a 2002 study published in the *American Journal of Clinical Nutrition*, A.] Raben et al. reported that obese subjects gained weight when they were given sucrose, primarily in the form of sugar-sweetened beverages, for 10 weeks, whereas they lost weight when they were given noncaloric sweeteners for the same length of time.

Four long-term, randomized, controlled trials examining the relationship between the consumption of sugar-sweetened beverages and body weight have been reported; the results showed the strongest effects among overweight persons. . . .

Diabetes and Heart Disease

Three prospective, observational studies—one involving nurses in the United States, one involving Finnish men and women, and one involving black women—each showed positive associations between the consumption of sugar-sweetened beverages and the risk of type 2 diabetes. Among the 91,249 women in the Nurses' Health Study II who were followed for 8 years, the risk of diabetes among women who consumed one or more servings of sugar-sweetened beverages per day was nearly double the risk among women who consumed less than one serving of sugar-sweetened beverages per month; about half the excess risk was accounted for by greater body weight. Among black women, excess weight accounted for most of the excess risk.

Among 88,520 women in the Nurses' Health Study, the risk of coronary heart disease among women who consumed one serving of sugar-sweetened beverages per day, as compared with women who consumed less than one serving per month, was increased by 23%, and among those who consumed two servings or more per day, the risk was increased by 35%. Increased body weight explained some, but not all, of this association.

How Soda Drinking Contributes to Poor Health

A variety of behavioral and biologic mechanisms may be responsible for the associations between the consumption of sugar-sweetened beverages and adverse health outcomes, with some links (e.g., the link between intake of sugar-sweetened beverages and weight gain) better established than others. The well-documented adverse physiological and metabolic consequences of a high intake of refined carbohydrates such as sugar include the elevation of triglyceride levels and of blood pressure and the lowering of high-density lipoprotein cholesterol levels, which would be expected to increase the risk of coronary heart disease. Because of the high glycemic load of sugar-sweetened beverages, consumption of these beverages would be expected to increase the risk of diabetes by causing insulin resistance and also through direct effects on pancreatic islet cells. Observational research has shown that consumption of sugar-sweetened beverages, but not of noncalorically sweetened beverages, is associated with markers of insulin resistance.

Intake of sugar-sweetened beverages may cause excessive weight gain owing in part to the apparently poor satiating properties of sugar in liquid form. Indeed, adjustment of caloric intake at subsequent meals for energy that had been consumed as a beverage is less complete than adjustment of intake for energy that had been consumed as a solid food. For example, in a study involving 323 adults, in which 7-day food diaries were used, energy from beverages added to total energy intake instead of displacing other sources of calories. The results of a study of school-age children were consistent with the data from adults and showed that children who drank 9 oz or more of sugar-sweetened beverages per day consumed nearly 200 kcal per day more than those who did not drink sugar-sweetened beverages.

Short-term studies of the effect of beverage consumption on energy intake support this mechanism. Among 33 adults who were given identical test lunches on six occasions but were given beverages of different types (sugar-sweetened cola, noncaloric cola, or water) and amounts (12 oz [355 ml] or 18 oz [532 ml]), the intake of solid food did not differ across conditions; the result was that there was significantly greater total energy consumption when the sugar-sweetened beverages were served.

Sugar-sweetened beverages may also affect body weight through other behavioral mechanisms. Whereas the intake of solid food is characteristically coupled to hunger, people may consume sugar-sweetened beverages in the absence of hunger, to satisfy thirst or for social reasons. Sugar-sweetened beverages may also have chronic adverse effects on taste preferences and food acceptance. Persons—especially children—who habitually consume sugar-sweetened beverages rather than water may find more satiating but less sweet foods (e.g., vegetables, legumes, and fruits) unappealing or unpalatable, with the result that their diet may be of poor quality.

Economic Reasons to Intervene

Economists agree that government intervention in a market is warranted when there are "market failures" that result in less-than-optimal production and consumption. Several market failures exist with respect to sugar-sweetened beverages. First, because many persons do not fully appreciate the links between consumption of these beverages and health consequences, they make consumption decisions with imperfect information. These decisions are likely to be further distorted by the extensive marketing campaigns that advertise the benefits of consumption. A second failure results from time-inconsistent preferences (i.e., decisions that provide short-term gratification but long-term harm). This problem is exacerbated in the case of children and adolescents, who place a higher value on present satisfaction while more heavily discounting future consequences. Finally, financial "externalities" exist in the market for sugar-sweetened beverages in that consumers do not bear the full costs of their consumption decisions. Because of the contribution of the consumption of sugar-sweetened beverages to obesity, as well as the health consequences that are independent of weight, the consumption of sugar-sweetened beverages generates excess health care costs. Medical costs for overweight and obesity alone are estimated to be $147 billion—or 9.1% of U.S. health care expenditures—with half these costs paid for publicly through the Medicare and Medicaid programs.

Selecting an Appropriate Tax and Tax Rate

Key factors to consider in developing an effective policy include the definition of taxable beverages, the type of tax (sales tax or excise tax), and the tax rate. We propose an excise tax of 1 cent per ounce for beverages that have any added caloric sweetener. An alternative would be to tax beverages that exceed a threshold of grams of added caloric sweetener or of kilocalories per ounce. If this approach were used, we would recommend that the threshold be set at 1 g [gram] of sugar per ounce (30 ml) (32 kcal per 8 oz [237 ml]). Another option would be a tax assessed per gram of added sugar, but such an approach would be difficult to administer. The advantage of taxing beverages that have any added sugar is that this kind of tax is simpler to administer and it may promote the consumption of no-calorie beverages, most notably water; however, a threshold approach would also promote calorie reductions and would encourage manufacturers to reformulate products. A consumer who drinks a conventional soft drink (20 oz [591 ml]) every day and switches to a beverage below this threshold would consume approximately 174 fewer calories each day.

A specific excise tax (a tax levied on units such as volume or weight) per ounce or per gram of added sugar would be preferable to a sales tax or an ad valorem excise tax (a tax levied as a percentage of price) and would provide an incentive to reduce the amount of sugar per ounce of a sugar-sweetened beverage. Sales taxes added as a percentage of retail cost would have three disadvantages: they could simply encourage the purchase of lower-priced brands (thus resulting in no calorie reduction) or of large containers that cost less per ounce; consumers would become aware of the added tax only after making the decision to purchase the beverage; and the syrups that are used in fountain drinks, which are often served with multiple refills, would remain untaxed. A number of states currently exempt sugar-sweetened beverages from sales taxes along with food, presumably because food is a necessity. This practice should be eliminated, whether or not an excise tax is enacted.

Excise taxes could be levied on producers and wholesalers, and the cost would almost certainly be passed along to retailers, who would then incorporate it into the retail price; thus, consumers would become aware of the cost at the point of making a purchase decision. Taxes levied on producers and wholesalers would be much easier to collect and enforce than taxes levied on retailers because of the smaller number of businesses that would have to comply with the tax; in addition, the sugar used in syrups could be taxed—a major advantage because of the heavy sales of fountain drinks. Experience with tobacco and alcohol taxes suggests that specific excise taxes have a greater effect on consumption than do ad valorem excise taxes and can also generate more stable revenues because they are less dependent on industry pricing strategies. In addition, tax laws should be written with provisions for the regular adjustment of specific excise taxes to keep pace with inflation, in order to prevent the effect of the taxes on both prices and revenues from eroding over time.

Expected Reduction in Consumption

A tax of 1 cent per ounce of beverage would increase the cost of a 20-oz soft drink by 15 to 20%. The effect on consumption can be estimated through research on price elasticity (i.e., consumption shifts produced by price). The price elasticity for all soft drinks is in the range of −0.8 to −1.0. (Elasticity of −0.8 suggests that for every 10% increase in price, there would be a decrease in consumption of 8%, whereas elasticity of −1.0 suggests that for every 10% increase in price, there would be a decrease in consumption of 10%.) Even greater price effects are expected from taxing only sugar-sweetened beverages, since some consumers will switch to diet beverages. With the use of a conservative estimate that consumers would substitute calories in other forms for 25% of the reduced calorie consumption, an excise tax of 1 cent per ounce would lead to a minimum reduction of 10% in calorie consumption from sweetened beverages, or 20 kcal per person per day, a reduction that is sufficient for weight loss and reduction in risk (unpublished data). The benefit would be larger among consumers who consume higher volumes, since these consumers are more likely to be overweight and appear to be more responsive to prices. Higher taxes would have greater benefits.

A controversial issue is whether to tax beverages that are sweetened with noncaloric sweeteners. No adverse health effects of noncaloric sweeteners have been consistently demonstrated, but there are concerns that diet beverages may increase calorie consumption by justifying consumption of other caloric foods or by promoting a preference for sweet tastes. At present, we do not propose taxing beverages with noncaloric sweeteners, but we recommend close tracking of studies to determine whether taxing might be justified in the future.

Potential Benefits and Concerns

The revenue generated from a tax on sugar-sweetened beverages would be considerable and could be used to help support childhood nutrition programs, obesity-prevention programs, or health care for the uninsured or to help meet general revenue needs. A national tax of 1 cent per ounce on sugar-sweetened beverages would raise $14.9 billion in the first year alone. Taxes at the state level would also generate considerable revenue—for example, $139 million in Arkansas, $183 million in Oregon, $221 million in Alabama, $928 million in Florida, $937 million in New York, $1.2 billion in Texas, and $1.8 billion in California. A tax calculator that is available online can generate revenue numbers for states and 25 major cities.

One objection to a tax on sugar-sweetened beverages is that it would be regressive [that is, it would take a larger percentage of income from poor people]. This argument arose with respect to tobacco taxes but was challenged successfully by proponents of the taxes, who pointed out that the poor face a disproportionate burden of smoking-related illnesses, that nearly all smokers begin to smoke when they are teenagers, and that both groups are sensitive to price changes. In addition, some of the tobacco revenue has been used for programs developed specifically for the poor and for youth. The poor are most affected by illnesses that are related to unhealthful diets, and brand loyalties for beverages tend to be set by the teenage years. In addition, sugar-sweetened beverages are not necessary for survival, and an alternative (i.e., water) is available at little or no cost; hence, a tax that shifted intake from sugar-sweetened beverages to water would benefit the poor both by improving health and by lowering expenditures on beverages. Designating revenues for programs promoting childhood nutrition, obesity prevention, or health care for the uninsured would preferentially help those most in need.

A second objection is that taxing sugar-sweetened beverages will not solve the obesity crisis and is a blunt instrument that affects even those who consume small amounts of such beverages. Seat-belt legislation and tobacco taxation do not eliminate traffic accidents and heart disease but are nevertheless sound policies. Similarly, obesity is unlikely to yield to any single policy intervention, so it is important to pursue multiple opportunities to obtain incremental gains. Reducing caloric intake by 1 to 2% per year would have a marked impact on health in all age groups, and the financial burden on those who consumed small amounts of sugar-sweetened beverages would be minimal.

| "Soda tax hikes are also unlikely to be large enough to significantly lower the weight of the population."

A Soda Tax Would Not Help Reduce Obesity

Michael L. Marlow and Alden F. Shiers

Michael L. Marlow and Alden F. Shiers are professors of economics at California Polytechnic State University. In the viewpoint that follows, Marlow and Shiers claim that a tax on sodas and other sugar-sweetened beverages is not the remedy to fight obesity. The pair concludes that the link between soda consumption and weight gain is not proven, and even if it were proven, Marlow and Shiers assert that a tax would be difficult to apply as well as unfair to those soda drinkers who do not suffer from obesity. Finally, Marlow and Shiers argue that a soda tax will likely push drinkers to find substitutes for sugar-sweetened beverages and thus not cure the problem.

As you read, consider the following questions:

1. What percentage of US soda sales is made up of regular (sugar-sweetened) soda, as Marlow and Shiers report?

Michael L. Marlow and Alden F. Shiers, "Would Soda Taxes Really Yield Health Benefits?" *Regulation*, Fall 2010. pp. 34–38. Copyright 2010 by American Enterprise Institute for Public Policy. Reproduced with permission of Cato Institute via Copyright Clearance Center.

2. In a paper published in *Contemporary Economic Policy* and cited by the authors, by what fraction do Jason Fletcher and colleagues believe a 58 percent tax on soda would drop the average body mass index?

3. Why do Marlow and Shiers doubt that a soda tax would be used to fund obesity prevention programs?

Roughly one-third of U.S. adults are classified as obese, which is defined as having a body mass index of 30 or higher. . . . Obesity is especially prevalent among minorities; African-Americans have a 51 percent higher prevalence of obesity, and Hispanics have 21 percent higher obesity prevalence than whites.

Obesity has become a major public health concern, given its association with chronic conditions that include diabetes, hypertension, high cholesterol, stroke, heart disease, certain cancers, and arthritis. Excess mortality stemming primarily from cardiovascular disease and diabetes is also believed to be associated with higher grades of obesity. Researchers at the Centers for Disease Control and Prevention in Atlanta estimate that obesity now accounts for 9.1 percent of all medical spending—$147 billion in 2008.

Various factors are believed to promote rising obesity rates, but the hypothesized relationship between "nutritively sweetened beverages" (NSBs) and obesity has increasingly become the focus of attention. Some public health advocates call for Pigouvian taxes [after economist Arthur Pigou] on these beverages, often referred to as "soda taxes," as effective interventions that will lower obesity as well as generate tax revenues that can be used to fund public programs aimed at lowering obesity.

In this [viewpoint], we discuss the economic theory and empirical evidence of using soda taxes to lower obesity. We conclude that these taxes are unlikely to significantly lower obesity, and that they promote many unintended consequences that may adversely affect public health. Higher tax revenues stemming from soda taxes are also likely to be used to expand government programs other than those associated with controlling obesity, much as cigarette tax revenue now does.

Questionable Assumptions Concerning a Soda Tax

Proponents of soda taxes argue for government intervention because, they say, free markets fail to allocate resources in soda markets efficiently, with the ultimate consequence being too many obese people. Three assumptions underlie their argument:

- Soda causes obesity.

- Consumers lack adequate information and beverage choices.

- Soda drinkers impose external costs on others who pick up some portion of obese people's higher medical costs.

Let us consider each of these assumptions.

The correlation between soda consumption and obesity rates does not imply that soda consumption causes obesity. Other possibilities include obesity causes soda consumption, no relationship exists between soda consumption and obesity, and soda consumption and obesity are interdependent. Moreover, even if soda consumption did cause obesity, there is no reason to believe that soda is the lone causal factor behind obesity; other likely candidates include lack of exercise, age, genetics, consumption of other high-calorie foods and beverages, and many other factors.

Tax advocates claim that soda consumption causes obesity, but evidence demonstrating this causal link is weak at best. A 2006 [*American Journal of Clinical Nutrition*] review article by Vasanti Malik et al.[1] of the relationship between the consumption of sugar-sweetened beverages and obesity found 16 studies indicating a significant positive relationship between consumption and body mass index, 10 studies that did not find a significant positive relationship, and four studies with mixed results. A 2007 [*American Journal of Public Health*] literature review by Lenny Vartanian et al. found eight studies with a significant positive relationship, 15 studies with no significant positive relationship, and two studies with mixed results.

Although the authors of these surveys conclude that the evidence supports the view that soda consumption causes obesity, we suggest the evidence remains less than clear. Most articles in their surveys demonstrate correlation and not causation, and ignore confounding factors such as age, exercise, genetics, and other factors that probably affect body weight. The Malik survey acknowledges this point:

> Overall, results from our review support a link between the consumption of sugar-sweetened beverages and the risks of overweight and obesity. However, interpretation of the published studies is complicated by several method-related issues, including small sample size, short duration of follow-up, lack of repeated measures of dietary exposures and outcomes, and confounding by other diet and lifestyle factors.

A recent commentary by David Allison and Richard Mattes in *JAMA: The Journal of the American Medical Association* acknowledges this same point:

> Given current evidence, little can be concluded with confidence beyond the fact that requiring individuals to drink large amounts of NSBs causes greater weight gain than not doing so. Randomized controlled trials of NSB consumption reduction have been applied effectiveness studies rather than rigorously controlled efficacy studies. Only the latter insures fidelity of the intervention.

The authors conclude that much of the research and subsequent news reports surrounding the issue have been extensively influenced by multiple biases that have eroded the reporting of objective science on this important public health matter.

The Role of Consumer Choice

Some soda tax advocates claim that consumers drink too much soda as a result of inadequate access to healthier food and beverage choices. But there are roughly 40,000 food products in the typical U.S. supermarket. It is difficult to argue that this array of products somehow ignores consumer preferences, especially given competitive pressures and technological advances in processing, storage, transportation, and communication.

The growing variety of food products reflects an industry that adapts to consumer preferences regarding health-related choices. Between 1987 and 2004, 35,272 new food products labeled "low fat" or "no fat" were introduced into the U.S. food market. That led researchers at the U.S. Department of Agriculture to conclude that unhealthy food consumption patterns do not stem from a market failure to supply healthy food and beverage choices.

While regular soda accounts for roughly 70 percent of U.S. soda sales, diet soda sales have been growing rapidly. Some forecasters predict that diet sales will eventually overtake regular soda. It thus seems that an active private market exists in providing "healthy" choices to consumers, which suggest that there is little need for government intervention into soda markets.

Figuring the Costs of Obesity

Soda tax advocates argue that negative externalities—external costs not fully accounted for in markets—indicate a market failure in which too much soda is consumed. Externalities are argued to exist because consumers who become obese will not fully pick up the higher medical costs associated with their obesity. Taxes equal to these external costs would theoretically raise soda prices to levels consistent with efficient consumption levels.

However, it is unlikely that taxes could ever correct for any externality associated with obesity. The problem with the externality argument is that, even if obesity raises health care costs of the obese, this externality should be corrected by having health insurers impose surcharges on obese insureds that reflect the additional costs. Few criticize surcharges imposed by auto insurance firms on drivers with drunk driving records, so why not correct for higher costs associated with obesity through insurance premiums?

Unfortunately, federal health care legislation passed earlier this year [2010] severely reduces or eliminates differential health insurance pricing. The legislation requires insurance companies to provide coverage for preventive health services, which include obesity screening and nutritional counseling. The legislation does not require obese people to pay more for insurance, but provisions could possibly allow insurers to charge premiums to people with "lifestyle risk factors" such as tobacco use. It remains doubtful that obesity will be considered a lifestyle risk, however, given the legislation's focus on obesity screening and nutritional counseling. Moreover, expected eliminations of preexisting exclusion clauses that previously allowed insurers to deny coverage to obese individuals and those with past bariatric surgery would reinforce the view that obesity is not a lifestyle risk factor that should be reflected in higher insurance premiums.

Still, it remains unclear that soda consumption causes obesity, or that it is the sole causal factor behind obesity. And even if it is, the sensible policy would be to alter health insurance premiums to allow for obesity risk premiums, not a Pi-

© John McPherson/Distributed by Universal Uclick via CartoonStock.com

"Instead of passing the fat tax on soda, the government requires that people do 10 chin-ups before the cooler will open," by John McPherson. www.CartoonStock.com.

gouvian tax on soda. Such reform would not rely on the false premise that soda consumption is the lone causal factor behind obesity, as such a risk premium would "tax" body weight, which is the essential problem that soda tax advocates claim they are interested in controlling. Yet we are not aware of any soda tax advocate who also supports adjusting health insurance premiums.

Finally, even if obesity shortens lives, economic theory indicates that obesity reflects a positive externality rather than a negative one. That is, external benefits associated with obesity are not fully accounted for in markets since obese individuals collect less from Medicare and Social Security over their shorter lifetimes. Kip Viscusi has estimated that smokers "save" taxpayers roughly 23¢–32¢ for each pack of cigarettes they smoke because of reduced social insurance costs—in addition to excise taxes already levied on cigarettes. A recent paper by K. McPherson analyzing United Kingdom data found that, although annual health care costs are highest for obese people earlier in life (until age 56 years), and are highest for smokers at older ages, the ultimate lifetime costs are highest for the healthy (nonsmoking, non-obese) people. McPherson finds that life expectancy from age 20 is reduced by five years for obese people and seven for smokers. The consequence is that healthy people live to incur greater medical expenditure on average, more than compensating for the earlier excess costs related to obesity or smoking.

Non-obese individuals thus receive external benefits in the form of additional public resources. If we were to follow soda tax advocates' thinking, then we should in fact subsidize soda consumption so as to encourage it. Despite tax advocates' fondness for taxing negative externalities, they never seem as anxious to correct positive externalities.

What Is the "Correct" Soda Tax?

Even if tax advocates are correct about soda consumption causing so many problems, it is unlikely that soda taxes would rectify the externality. The distance between theory and practice in the real world is great enough to warrant much skepticism over the ability of policy makers to calculate the "correct" tax and then implement it in a world where politics and special interests have vested interests in designing tax codes.

Policy makers must legislate "correct" taxes to truly correct externalities. Since it remains unclear that soda consumption causes obesity or whether it reflects negative or positive externalities, the possible range of "correct" soda taxes lies between positive, zero, and negative values. Thus, it is unclear if obesity should be taxed, subsidized, or simply left alone, although tax advocates assume it should be taxed. Even if they are correct, the probability that policy makers know the correct tax is slim to none, thus leading to further possibilities that the tax is set too high, causing further erosion of resource efficiency.

Economic theory also indicates that, if there are negative externalities, taxes should vary over different beverages as well as different groups of consumers. Studies imply that the effects of NSBs on obesity differ for different types of drinks and, because different racial/ethnic groups have different preferences, that taxes should vary between groups. As noted above, the prevalence of obesity is highest for non-Hispanic blacks, followed by Hispanics, and then non-Hispanic whites. In addition, consumption data reveal that white persons consume more carbonated soft drinks than other racial/ethnic groups, and that blacks consume more high-calorie fruit drinks and ades [lemonade, limeade, orangeade, etc.]. If NSBs are a major cause of obesity, then these data suggest that fruit drinks and ades are a greater cause of obesity than carbonated soft drinks, and therefore fruit drinks and ades should be subjected to a higher tax than carbonated soft drinks. Yet there are no estimates of how much greater are the externalities of fruit drinks and ades than carbonated soft drinks, so there is no basis for determining the correct taxes. It is also unlikely that differential taxation across racial/ethnic groups would be legislated, thus again calling into question the ability of policy makers to "correctly" tax beverages for various externalities.

Unfairly Applied and Insignificant in Reducing Obesity

Although common sense indicates that not all soda drinkers are obese or even overweight, a soda tax cannot differentiate between consumers by their weight. Even if soda consumption causes obesity, there is no logic to taxing consumers—even excessive ones—who do not have weight problems.

Moreover, taxes on all soda consumers are likely to exert differential effects on light vs. heavy demanders. A recent study finds that taxes on alcohol consumption significantly lower drinking by light drinkers, but not heavy drinkers. Thus, taxes dramatically lower consumption of those who drink relatively little, but exert little to no effect on consumption habits of those individuals who are the targets of policy makers. There is little reason to suspect anything different in the case of soda taxes.

Soda tax hikes are also unlikely to be large enough to significantly lower the weight of the population. A recent [2010 *Contemporary Economic Policy*] paper by Jason Fletcher et al. examined how state tax rate changes from 1990 to 2006 affected body mass index. They found that a one percentage point increase in the tax rate was associated with a decrease of just 0.003 points in body mass. Thus, even a large tax increase is unlikely to exert much effect on population weight. The authors concluded, for example, that a 58 percent tax on soda, equivalent to the average federal and state tax on cigarettes, would drop the average body mass by only 0.16 points—a trivial effect given that obesity is defined as a body mass index of at least 30. Thus, it is most unlikely that taxes could be raised enough to transform the obese into much slimmer people.

Consumers Will Find Substitutes

Unintended consequences of government intervention arise whether or not its advocates wish to acknowledge them. Economic theory demonstrates that taxes focused on one product, such as soda, will lead consumers to purchase substitutes. What beverages and food consumers would switch to and what the social effects of that change would be are not known.

Soda tax advocates seem to believe that a soda tax will lead to more water and diet drink consumption, but it is likely that substitutions into other products with caloric properties similar to soda will arise, with overall effects on weight unknown. Moreover, a supply of new drink choices is likely to emerge that creatively circumvents the new taxes, thus again muting intended reductions in sugar consumption.

Examples of unintended consequences of interventions abound. A 2004 [*Journal of Health Economics*] study by M.C. Farrelly et al. and a 2006 [*American Economic Review*] study by J. Adda and F. Cornaglia both indicate that tax hikes on cigarettes have led smokers to switch to higher tar and nicotine brands so that they can maintain chemical intake levels as they smoke less, to the detriment of their health. A 2001 [*Journal of Health Economics*] study by John DiNardo and Thomas Lemieux found that teen marijuana consumption rose following state tax increases on beer. A 2004 [*Journal of Health Economics*] study by S.Y. Chou et al. found that higher cigarette prices, which reduce smoking, are associated with higher rates of obesity.

Recent research suggests a few of the unintended consequences of soda taxes. Some consumers will likely switch to diet sodas, but some researchers worry that the health effects of artificial sweeteners may be worse than those of regular sugar. A recent [2009 *Journal of Public Economics*] study by Gideon Yaniv et al. concludes that a tax on junk food (including soda) could increase obesity as it leaves less time for exercise, especially among physically active people, when it leads them to spend more time shopping for fresh ingredients and preparing food at home.

A Soda Tax Cannot Remedy
All Obesity Factors

Recent economic research indicates that factors other than soda are probable causal factors of obesity. A 2003 [*Perspectives in Biology and Medicine*] study by Tomas Philipson and Richard Posner finds that technological change has reduced the demands for heavy labor and thus created a more sedentary workforce prone to weight gain. Another 2003 [*Journal of Economic Perspectives*] study by David Cutler et al. points out that improvements in food-storage technology have reduced the time cost of preparing meals, which leads to more food and beverage consumption. Finally, huge innovations in medical technology that include treatment of obesity-related illnesses have arisen that lessen health-related costs of obesity. As a result, some people have become less concerned about their weight. It remains unclear how a soda tax would overturn any of these factors that contribute to weight gain.

Failure of Good Intentions

Despite good intentions or political promises to the contrary, past efforts to fund prevention programs often fund very little of those programs. Tobacco control is a clear example of where promises failed to meet practice. It has been estimated that no more than 10 cents on the dollar of funds from the 1998 Master Settlement Agreement with tobacco companies have been spent on tobacco control programs, despite promises that a majority of the funds would be aimed at smoking prevention. Given the current fiscal imbalances at the state and federal levels, increased tax revenues generated through soda taxes would surely have a similar fate. Moreover, spending on tobacco control has been shown to exert trivial effects on cigarette consumption, thus calling into question the effectiveness of public spending on obesity prevention efforts.

We have argued that soda taxes are unlikely to correct for any real or imagined problems related to our nation's obesity rate. It is not only unclear that soda causes obesity, but even if it did, policy makers have neither the technical expertise nor political courage to set taxes that correct any externality problems.

Even if policy makers did have such expertise, soda taxes would likely be regressive, as lower-income households spend a greater share of their income on soda than higher-income households. As such, soda taxes would disproportionately fall on the poor—soda drinkers who may or may not be obese. If non-obese individuals truly pay some of the higher health care costs of the obese, the best solution would be to correct this negative externality through imposing surcharges on health insurance premiums of the obese.

Periodical Bibliography

The following articles have been selected to supplement the diverse views presented in this chapter.

Julian M. Alston et al.   "Likely Effects on Obesity from Proposed Changes to the US Food Stamp Program," *Food Policy*, April 2009.

John Cawley   "The Economics of Childhood Obesity," *Health Affairs*, March 2010.

Barbara Kiviat   "Tax and Sip," *Time*, July 12, 2010.

Jay E. Maddock   "Soda Taxes, Obesity, and the Perils of Complexity," *American Journal of Health Promotion*, November–December 2010.

Bidisha Mandal   "Use of Food Labels as a Weight Loss Behavior," *Journal of Consumer Affairs*, Fall 2010.

N. Gregory Mankiw   "Can a Soda Tax Save Us from Ourselves?" *New York Times*, June 5, 2010.

Michael Tennant   "Michelle Obama's Federal Fat Farm," *New American*, August 31, 2010.

Bijal Trivedi   "The Calorie Delusion: Why Food Labels Are Wrong," *New Scientist*, July 15, 2009.

OPPOSING
VIEWPOINTS®
SERIES

CHAPTER 3

What Societal Factors Influence Nutrition?

Chapter Preface

Since the 1980s, when obesity became a national concern, various health experts, lawmakers, and social commentators have questioned what factors in American culture may be contributing to the fattening of the population. Correlations, though, are difficult to determine, and some observers are hesitant to pinpoint specific relationships between personal or social behaviors and weight gain. The US Department of Health and Human Services, for example, records that various trends among young people—such as eating away from home more often, snacking, and the unregulated consumption of sugared drinks—"suggest some changes in eating patterns and consumption . . . may be correlated with increases in obesity." Other organizations cite the prevalence of fast food in America's diet in addition to the consumption of larger, high-calorie meals as causal factors. Such habits seem to be part of a broader change in living styles—including more sedentary pursuits and less physical activity—that may promote poor nutrition and unchecked weight gain.

Many health researchers, though, add that trends in obesity may be due to a mix of behaviors, circumstances, and biology. In a September 18, 2010, *Huffington Post* column, physician and wellness author Mark Hyman argued that food scarcity among America's poor was plumping up that segment of society. Without the financial resources to buy more expensive, healthier foods, cash-strapped individuals and families are finding unhealthy alternatives. "For a large portion of Americans floating on or sinking beneath the poverty line this means bingeing on cheap, sugary, starchy, fatty calories in order to avoid hunger," Hyman claims. At the other end of the spectrum of causes, some scientists maintain that circumstance may contribute to overeating, but the desire to consume and achieve a specific body weight may be hardwired into the genetic makeup of each individual. According to a *Newsweek* article published on the magazine's website on September 10, 2009, "Genetic studies have shown that the particular set of weight-regulating genes that a person has is by far the most important factor in determining how much that person will weigh. The heritability of obesity—a measure of how much obesity is due to genes versus other factors—is about the same as the heritability of height." Such findings suggest that the way to counter obesity may be through genetic therapies rather than crash dieting.

In the following chapter, analysts examine some of the societal culprits most commonly blamed for engendering obesity and weight gain. Drawing a relationship between these influences and obesity implies that altering them may help resolve the problem. However, whether these perceived social failings are the most pressing factors contributing to obesity is still a subject of equally unresolved debate.

*"School lunches today meet federal nu-
trition standards and serve more fresh
fruits and vegetables, whole grains and
low-fat dairy than ever before."*

School Lunch Programs
Encourage Proper Nutrition

School Nutrition Association

*The School Nutrition Association (SNA) is a national nonprofit
organization of professionals working in the school dietary and
nutrition field. In the following viewpoint, the SNA claims that
school-prepared meals provide about one-third of the necessary
daily nutrition requirements for students. Refuting several myths
that school meals are rife with junk foods, the SNA asserts that
all meals meet government standards and typically contain more
healthy choices than meals brought from home. Furthermore, the
organization claims that students who eat school meals tend to
maintain healthier weights than those who do not.*

As you read, consider the following questions:

1. According to established dietary guidelines cited by the
   SNA, no more than what percentage of calories in a
   school-prepared lunch can come from fat?

School Nutrition Association, "Beyond the Stereotypes: Facts About School Lunches,"
School Nutrition Association, March 10, 2008. Copyright © 2011 by School Nutrition
Association. Reproduced by permission.

2. As the SNA attests, how do school lunch programs attempt to make a food item like pizza a healthy choice?

3. How is the sale of soda regulated in schools, as the SNA reports?

Media reports about school lunches often omit the facts and perpetuate out-dated stereotypes and biased information about school nutrition programs.

School lunches today meet federal nutrition standards and serve more fresh fruits and vegetables, whole grains and low-fat dairy than ever before. On a very tight budget, school nutrition professionals are preparing and serving balanced, nutritious meals in age-appropriate portion sizes that provide critical nutrients and promote a healthy childhood weight.

What Do "School Meals" Consist Of? Get the Facts!

Under the National School Lunch Program (NSLP) and the School Breakfast Program (SBP), school meals are required to meet federal nutrition standards limiting fat, saturated fat and portion size and requiring that every school lunch include milk, fruits and vegetables, a grain and a protein. In return, schools receive a reimbursement for each meal served.

The Healthy, Hunger-Free Kids Act (Public Law 111-296) passed in December 2010 required the US Department of Agriculture (USDA) to strengthen these federal nutrition standards. In January 2011, USDA released proposed nutrition standards including new calorie and sodium limits, larger fruit and vegetable serving sizes and requirements to expand the variety of vegetables served in schools each week. The standards will be finalized in 2012, but schools are already working toward these goals.

Currently, "competitive foods" sold in à la carte lines, snack bars, school stores and other venues during the school day, are not required to meet these stringent nutrition standards. However, Public Law 111-296 called on USDA to develop new nutrition standards for competitive foods. USDA is expected to release proposed standards by December 2011 and final regulations by the summer of 2013.

Schools Do Not Serve Junk Food

Below are several popular misconceptions about school meals and the truth behind the myths.

Myth #1: School meals make children obese.

Fact: Research has shown that students who eat meals served through the National School Lunch Program (NSLP) are more likely to be at a healthy weight. A study published in the August 2003 issue of *Archives of Pediatrics & Adolescent Medicine* concluded that "girls in food-insecure households had significantly reduced odds of being at risk of overweight if they participated in the [National School Lunch, School Breakfast and food stamp programs]." The research highlights the importance of food assistance programs to low-income children not only in addressing hunger "but also in potentially protecting them from excess weight gain."[i]

NSLP participants are more likely than non-participants to consume vegetables, milk and milk products, and meat and other protein-rich foods, both at lunch and over 24 hours; they also consume less soda and/or fruit drinks.[ii] Additionally, researchers from the Ohio State University and Indiana University released a study in spring 2007 that indicated children are more likely to gain weight during the summer months as opposed to during the school year. The research indicates that influences other than school meal programs could be responsible for increases in childhood overweight.

Myth #2: Schools serve junk food for school lunch.

Fact: Meals served under the National School Lunch Program (NSLP) must, by federal law, meet nutrition guidelines based on the Dietary Guidelines for Americans. No more than 30 percent of calories can come from fat and less than 10 percent from saturated fat. School lunches must provide one-third of the Recommended Dietary Allowances of protein, vitamin A, vitamin C, iron, calcium and calories. These guidelines apply over the course of one week of school lunch menus.

The 2007 *School Nutrition Dietary Assessment III* (SNDA III) study based on research by the US Department of Agriculture during the 2004–2005 school year found that in about 90 percent of all schools nationwide, students had opportunities to select low-fat lunch options. Additionally more than 70 percent of schools studied served meals that provided all the nutrients students need for healthy lifestyles, including protein, iron, calcium, and vitamins A and C. In fact, NSLP participants consumed more of six key nutrients at lunch than non-participants. NSLP participation is associated with higher average intakes of many nutrients, both at lunch and over 24 hours. Participants also have substantially lower intakes of added sugars than do non-participants.[iii]

Serving Recommended Portions of Nutritious Food

Myth #3: Schools don't serve enough fruits or vegetables for lunch.

Fact: According to the *School Nutrition Dietary Assessment III*, the median number of all fruit and vegetable options (including canned fruit and cooked vegetables) offered over the course of a week was 13 in secondary schools.[iii] The *2009 School Nutrition Operations Report: [The State of School Nutrition 2009]* conducted by School Nutrition Association (SNA) found that fresh fruits and vegetables are offered daily in 98.8 percent of school districts.[iv] Furthermore, salad bars or pre-packaged salads are offered in 91 percent of districts.[iv] Vegetarian options are served in 63.9 percent of school districts, according to the 2009 SNA operations report.

Myth #4: Schools serve fried, greasy foods.

Fact: Schools may serve french fries, chicken nuggets or pizza at times. However, meals are required to meet the Recommended Dietary Allowances and federal nutrition standards, including limits on fat and saturated fat. As a result, these options are often baked, not fried, made with low-fat or lean ingredients, and served with vegetables, fruit and other options that make each meal balanced and nutritious. Pizza often has reduced fat cheese and whole grain crust, chicken patties and tenders are often baked and coated in whole grain breading. Increasingly, school french fries are baked, made from sweet potatoes or are oven-baked potato wedges.

Myth #5: Sack lunches from home are better than school meals.

Fact: Research by Dr. Alice Jo Rainville of Eastern Michigan University concluded that students who eat school lunches consume fewer calories from fat than students who bring their lunch from home. Furthermore, the research found school lunches contain three times as many dairy products, twice as much fruit and seven times the vegetable amounts as lunches brought from home.[v]

Schools Work Hard to Keep Junk Food Out

Myth #6: Soda is served with school lunch.

Fact: Federal law prohibits the sale of soda in the cafeteria during the school lunch period. State and local regulations may further prohibit the sale of soda before or after the lunch period or in other locations on the school campus. The federal nutrition standards currently being developed for competitive foods will likely further restrict the sale of full calorie sodas during the school day.

Myth #7: Only junk food is available through à la carte lines and vending machines.

Fact: While federal nutrition standards for these competitive foods and beverages are still being developed, many school districts and the states have implemented their own nutrition standards for these items.

In 2004, Congress required every school district to develop local wellness policies regarding food available in school, nutrition education, physical activity programs and other health programs. As a result, in many school districts, school nutrition professionals have joined with parents, students and other school stakeholders to implement nutrition guidelines for all foods and beverages sold on school campuses.

School Nutrition Association's 2010 Back to School Trends survey found that nearly two-thirds of districts with à la carte services are implementing nutrition standards and limiting the size and/or weight of their à la carte food and beverage offerings. Meanwhile, more than two-thirds of districts with vending services are increasing the availability of healthier beverages in vending machines.

Myth #8: What is served at schools is out of my control.

Fact: You can become active in setting policies at the local level! Join your local school wellness committee, school board, or PTA; write a letter and voice what you think schools should offer students. Wellness is a community effort and needs everyone's support. School nutrition professionals are committed to providing safe and nutritious meals to all children. Parents are encouraged to visit their student's cafeteria, try a lunch and talk to their school food service director about the nutritional profile of foods served.

Notes

i. "Jones et al., Lower Risk of Overweight in School-aged Food Insecure Girls Who Participate in Food Assistance," *Archives of Pediatrics & Adolescent Medicine*, August 2003.

ii. Mathematica Policy Research, Inc., Final report submitted to the US Department of Agriculture, *Children's Diets in the Mid-1990s. Dietary Intake and Its Relationship with School Meal Participation*, 2001.

iii. US Department of Agriculture, *School Nutrition and Dietary Assessment III*, November 2007.

iv. School Nutrition Association, *2009 School Nutrition Operations Report*, August 2009.

v. A. Rainville, "Nutritional Quality of Reimbursable School Lunches Compared to Lunches Brought from Home," *The Journal of Child Nutrition and Management*, Spring 2001.

| "As odd as it sounds, one of the key con-
tributors to poor nutrition in
schools—at least indirectly—may be
the National School Lunch Program."

School Lunch Programs May Encourage Poor Nutrition

Adam Bornstein

In the viewpoint that follows, Adam Bornstein claims school lunch programs are failing to encourage proper nutrition habits in students. According to the author, schools are trying to meet government nutrition standards, but the cost of doing so is depleting school treasuries. To make up for the shortfall, many schools feel compelled to offer à la carte items and vending machine snacks that are popular, empty-calorie foods, Bornstein writes. He also blames government academic agendas for stressing math, science, and reading at the expense of teaching health and nutrition. If younger generations are going to acquire healthier eating habits, Bornstein argues, then the government must pass sweeping reform to assist schools in providing better lunches and to eliminate junk food from school premises. Adam Bornstein is the fitness editor for Men's Health *magazine.*

Adam Bornstein, "Why Are Schools Selling Junk Food to Kids?" *Men's Health*, vol. 23, no. 9, November 2008. pp. 158–164. Copyright © 2008 by Rodale, Inc. All rights reserved. Reproduced by permission.

As you read, consider the following questions:

1. How does Bornstein define foods of "minimum nutritional value"?

2. How much of a financial deficit do America's schools run to provide for the 29.6 million children participating in the NSLP, according to Bornstein?

3. Why does Bornstein fault the No Child Left Behind Act for contributing to the problem of poor nutrition in schools?

It's no secret that childhood obesity is a major problem in America's schools. What's so baffling, though, is that despite our awareness, it's a *growing* problem. After all, one solution seems obvious and simple: Pull the plug on vending machines, ban junk food on campuses, and serve only healthy fare in cafeterias. Case closed, right? If only it were that easy.

"The government system is forcing our schools to choose," says Katie Wilson, Ph.D., president of the School Nutrition Association, a nonprofit organization dedicated to improving school meals and nutrition. "Schools can either provide only healthy foods and go into debt, or allow unhealthy options, which generate revenue but are also a contributing factor to weight gain."

This unappetizing proposition, says Wilson, is the result of education budget cuts and a flawed system. But while it may be hard to swallow, it's just one piece of the puzzle. That's because, well, French fries taste good. So do candy bars, potato chips, and soda. "Unless kids are properly educated, they're going to choose junk over healthy food at school and at home," says Wilson. "Unfortunately, the number one question children ask me about nutrition is, 'Why don't schools teach us right from wrong?'"

We wondered that, too. We also wanted to know how, exactly, a system meant to help kids is ultimately making them fat.

The Economics of Providing Healthy Meals

As odd as it sounds, one of the key contributors to poor nutrition in schools—at least indirectly—may be the National School Lunch Program (NSLP). Established in 1946, this federally subsidized program provides calorie-balanced meals at cost to all children, or at reduced or no cost to children in low-income families. The intention, of course, is to give every child access to an inexpensive, healthy lunch. And to ensure that this goal is met, the USDA [US Department of Agriculture] has set these basic nutrition standards for schools to follow.

All meals must provide one-third of the Recommended Dietary Allowance (RDA) for calories, protein, vitamin A, vitamin C, iron, and calcium. This makes sense, considering that children consume 19 percent to 50 percent of their daily calories in the school cafeteria, according to the USDA.

The meals must also match the USDA's Dietary Guidelines for Americans, which limit the fat content of a meal to 30 percent of total calories and cap saturated fat at less than 10 percent.

The program forbids foods of "minimum nutritional value" from being served inside the school cafeteria at mealtimes. These are items that provide less than 5 percent of eight specific nutrients—i.e., "empty-calorie" foods such as gum, soda, and jelly beans, which are primarily sugar.

All of which sounds sensible, but plenty of loopholes exist, particularly in that last requirement: Turns out, foods of minimum nutritional value, while not allowed for sale in the cafeteria, can be sold anywhere else in the school—for instance, from a vending machine on the way to the lunchroom. What's more, candy bars, chips, and doughnuts actually avoid the foods-of-minimum-value designation. (A main ingredient in many of these foods is refined flour, which by federal law is fortified with vitamins and minerals.) As a result, they can be sold in the lunchroom, side by side with healthier options. Of course, that's only if the schools choose to do so. And that leads to the bigger issue: dollars and cents.

"Schools lose money every day because it costs more money to prepare meals than the reimbursement they get from the federal government," says Donald Schumacher, M.D., medical director for the Center for Nutrition and Preventive Medicine, in Charlotte, North Carolina. Case in point: In 2008, the government increased the NSLP subsidy to schools, to $2.57 per meal per student, but the cost to prepare the lunches rose to $2.88. And while schools that purchase foods directly from the USDA receive an additional 20 cents per meal, they're still at an 11-cent deficit.

That amount might seem trivial, but multiply it by the 29.6 million children participating in the NSLP and it comes out to a daily nationwide deficit of $3.2 million. For perspective, a middle school with 1,000 students would be $19,800 in the hole after just 1 year.

Competitive Foods Make Money

Schools can raise prices, of course, and some are being forced to do so. But Wilson says this strategy leads to other problems: It defeats the purpose of providing low-cost, healthy meals in the first place, and it can also result in fewer kids purchasing the nutritionally balanced lunches.

The upshot is that schools have instead turned to offering "competitive foods." These items aren't part of the NSLP. They include foods of minimal nutrition—which can be sold in vending machines, school stores, and snack bars—as well as foods that don't meet other USDA guidelines but that can be offered à la carte in the cafeteria. This is where the trouble really begins. For instance, students buy competitive foods in greater proportions than the USDA-approved meals, taking away from their consumption of fruits and vegetables, according to a report to Congress presented by the Center for Science in the Public Interest [in 2001]. So while the NSLP helps schools serve healthy food, it has also opened the door to options that undermine that effort.

"Without full funding from the government, schools are being pinched, and we need a quick way to make money," says Wilson. "That's why we have vending machines. That's why we sell à la carte. And that's why we purchase unhealthy foods along with healthy foods. They're cheaper than the healthier foods, and we can turn a greater profit."

Only Some Schools Are Working on Healthier Food Choices

With 71 schools and 64,000 students, Volusia County, Florida, is one of the largest school districts in the country. And when it comes to instituting nutrition reform, it's also one of the most progressive. "Schools have a responsibility to address healthy eating and fitness," says district superintendent Margaret Smith. "And we're determined to protect the health of our students."

So despite a crisis that has forced the closing of several schools, Smith's district has instituted policies to ensure that fresh fruit, vegetables, and whole grains are offered in all schools on a regular basis. At the elementary level, signs are placed throughout cafeterias encouraging students to make healthy food choices, and water is placed at eye level in vending machines to compete with sports drinks. Soda is permitted only in high schools and only after the lunch hour is over. And this year [2008], one school in the district, Pierson Elementary, was among 43 schools nationally recognized for their promotion of healthy initiatives.

But Volusia administrators openly admit that the problems haven't been eliminated entirely. For example, some high school students still have easy access to vending machines throughout the buildings after lunch is over. "Vending machines provide revenue that helps fund extracurricular activities for students," says Joan Young, the school district's director of cafeteria services. This is one way the district manages to keep athletic programs afloat in the midst of big budget cuts.

And while healthy dishes are readily available in Volusia schools, the cafeteria also stocks what many teenagers would consider more desirable options, including chocolate cake, cookies, and pizza.

But remember, Volusia is working hard to fix these flaws. Many school districts across the country aren't so proactive. And all of these issues are compounded by the soaring cost of food due to high oil prices and a weak dollar. "I've been working in the food industry for 30 years and I've never seen price increases like the ones we've experienced over the past 18 months," says Bob Bloomer, regional vice president of Chartwells-Thompson, a subsidy of Compass Group, the largest food distributor in the world.

Even small price fluctuations can have a major impact: A five-cent increase in the price of milk will cost the Volusia school district an additional $750,000 in the 2008–2009 school year. And Young has especially noticed price increases for the so-called healthiest items, such as whole wheat bread and products with less sugar.

"The minute you say 'healthy,' it costs more," says Bloomer. "When you say 'zero trans fat,' it costs more. It's the nature of the beast." In Albany County School District 1 in Laramie, Wyoming, margarine with no trans fat costs 262 percent more than the option with trans fat, leading the schools to use the less healthy version. "There are some districts that just don't have the money. They don't care about whole wheat. They don't care about trans fat. And when I say they don't care, I mean they just can't afford it," says Bloomer.

Cutting Costs Through Easy Preparation

The [National School Lunch Program] law mandated that schools serve a mix of proteins, grains, fruits, vegetables and dairy, but with so many loopholes and perverse incentives, it never really required wholesome food, and after waves of budget cuts, many schools couldn't afford it.

Big food manufacturers offered an easy solution: cheap, frozen kid favorites—fast food, essentially, but USDA [US Department of Agriculture]-approved—that schools could simply warm and serve. Over time, cafeterias adapted to the food supply. Today, few are equipped for cooking from scratch.

Douglas McGray, "The War Over America's Lunch,"
Time, April 26, 2010.

In the end, superintendents and the school board are left with a dilemma: Find new ways to raise millions of dollars, or buy the types of foods students will purchase. "School administrators know that foods of minimum nutritional value provide a profit margin that makes up for what they're losing from the federally mandated meal," says Dr. Schumacher. "And these products can even give them a little bit of profit to put back into the school. Where is their incentive to stop that?"

A National Reform Is Needed

Make no mistake: Many schools are trying, according to the School Nutrition Association. In fact, 71 percent of them have attempted to make "significant" efforts to offer healthy food choices on their menus. And several states now ban vending machines in elementary schools or limit what can be sold in the machines and when students can access them. But clearly, it's going to take sweeping national reform to repair this problem.

New legislation is a good place to start, says Dr. Schumacher. He's working hard to push a bill ... that will hopefully help build momentum for improving children's nutrition in schools nationwide. The proposal is an update to the Child Nutrition Act of 1966. It uses current nutrition science to rewrite the definition of foods of minimum nutritional value and requires that they be removed from schools, effectively eliminating a multitude of unhealthy options. "The issue isn't about removing children's ability to make choices, it's about providing healthy options and making it harder for them to access bad foods," says Dr. Schumacher.

Research has shown that this strategy, along with education, can help. In a recent Temple University study of grades four through six, researchers removed all sodas, sweetened drinks, and snacks that didn't meet USDA nutrition standards from vending machines and cafeteria lines in five Philadelphia schools. They also implemented 50 hours of nutrition education for students and encouraged parents to purchase healthy snacks for their kids to eat at home. After 2 years, half as many of these kids became overweight, compared with kids in similar schools without the program.

While those numbers are encouraging, they also underscore the daunting challenge of overcoming childhood obesity. Sure, the study results sound impressive. But some of that is nifty data crunching—7.5 percent of the children in the prevention program packed on too many pounds, compared with 15 percent of the group that made no changes. Still, we have to start somewhere. And there's little doubt that a combination of approaches is necessary. "If you don't teach kids what's good and what's bad, you don't solve a whole lot by restricting things," says Wilson. "Education is our fat burner."

One barrier is the No Child Left Behind Act [of 2001]. Designed to improve the quality of education in public schools, it puts tremendous pressure on schools to ensure that students perform well on standardized tests in math and science. But as a result, physical education and health classes have been minimized—crippled, even—since tests aren't given in those subject areas.

So while some form of nutrition education is offered in many schools, it's very limited because the government doesn't see it as a priority.

"Until more money for federally funded school food programs and a mandate for nutrition education are in place, we'll always be in this situation," says Wilson. "We need major support from our national government."

Making Informed Consumers of the Next Generation

Interestingly, there may be a parallel between today's childhood obesity epidemic and the youth smoking problem from the 1970s, says Marlene Schwartz, Ph.D., the director of research and school programs for the Rudd Center for Food Policy and Obesity at Yale University. Back then, Schwartz recalls, no one thought the situation would improve. But as education matched preventive measures, children became informed and behaviors changed.

A 2007 University of Michigan study found that only 22 percent of high school seniors said they had smoked a cigarette in the previous 30 days, compared to 1976 when the number was 39 percent.

The big changes didn't begin, though, until the mid-1990s, when the government began to make it more difficult for the tobacco industry to target America's youth, according to the report.

Dr. Schumacher has seen the impact of this type of childrens' nutrition education in the research he's conducted.

"Recently, one of our children went home for dinner and saw his father pouring ketchup all over his food," recalls Dr. Schumacher. "This fourth-grade kid took the bottle and said, 'Dad, you need to read this label. Look how much sugar you just put on that.' And I thought, *Wow*."

Children answering health questions rather than asking them? Maybe that's the true solution to the obesity epidemic.

> *"Several studies have demonstrated that television ads do indeed have an effect—and not a good effect—on what children eat."*

Marketing Food to Children Leads Them to Eat Non-Nutritious Foods

Jane E. Brody

Jane E. Brody is a personal health columnist for the New York Times. *In the following viewpoint, she contends that advertising high-sugar or empty-calorie foods to children influences them to consume more of these unhealthy foods. As Brody writes, not all food companies, restaurants, and other venues have strict guidelines on what can and cannot be marketed to children, and most of these businesses recognize that their advertising has a powerful impact on children's food choices. To redress this problem, Brody advocates that parents make their concerns known to companies regarding what she sees as an "insidious" form of marketing.*

Jane E. Brody, "Risks for Youths Who Eat What They Watch," *New York Times*, April 19, 2010, p. 7. Copyright © 2010 The New York Times. All rights reserved. Used by permission and protected by the Copyright Laws of the United States. The printing, copying, redistribution, or retransmission of this Content without express written permission is prohibited.

As you read, consider the following questions:

1. How many food and entertainment companies failed the March 2010 Center for Science in the Public Interest grade report concerning marketing to children, as Brody reports?

2. According to the Center for Science in the Public Interest study, what percentage of food companies did not have at least some sort of policy about marketing to children?

3. In the *Pediatrics* report cited by the author, what percentage of the beverages shown in the 138 kids' movies surveyed were sugar-sweetened brands?

Many factors influence children's food choices: where they eat; what their friends and siblings eat; what parents eat and drink and bring into the house; what is served at school; and, of course, what they like.

But if you are a parent, would you want your children's food and beverage choices determined by manufacturers whose primary goal is to make money by getting them hooked on products of questionable nutritional value? The issue is of particular importance now that rates of childhood obesity are soaring throughout the country, influenced in no small way by commercial interests.

Too Much Sugar on TV

Last month [March 2010], the Center for Science in the Public Interest, a Washington-based advocacy group, gave a grade of F to 95 of 128 food and entertainment companies for their policies—or lack thereof—on marketing to children. This despite the Children's Food and Beverage Advertising Initiative started in 2006 by the [Council of] Better Business Bureaus, in which 16 major food and restaurant companies, representing about 80 percent of television food advertising expenditures, announced they would not market foods to children under 12 if they did not meet the companies' own nutritional standards.

Unfortunately, there's the rub. What a company like Kellogg's regards as an acceptable amount of sugar in a serving of breakfast cereal may not be what a nutrition-wise parent would choose. The cutoff adopted by Kellogg's is 12 grams (3 teaspoons of sugar), which would keep them from promoting Cocoa Krispies (14 grams of sugar in a one-cup serving) to children. But Frosted Flakes, with 11 grams, could still be advertised in venues where children 6 and older will see them. (The company does not aim advertising at children under 6.)

Also, since each company sets its own guidelines, what applies to Kellogg's might not apply to products made by General Mills or Post.

Many Ad Venues Do Not Have a Policy Regarding Children

"Despite the industry's self-regulatory system, the vast majority of food and entertainment companies have no protections in place for children," said Margo G. Wootan, the center's nutrition policy director. In the center's analysis of marketing to children, released last November, the highest grade, a B-plus, went to the candy maker Mars, which does not market to children under 12 and avoids other gimmicks that attract them.

"If companies were marketing bananas and broccoli, we wouldn't be concerned," Dr. Wootan said. "But instead, most marketing is for sugary cereals, fast food, snack foods and candy. And this junk-food marketing is a major contributor to childhood obesity."

Furthermore, the analysis showed, although 64 percent of food companies that advertise to children at least have some

Limit TV Time to Cut Calorie Intake

Although children and youth are encouraged to watch what they eat, many youth seem to eat what they watch, and in the process increase their risk for increasing their energy intake. In the absence of regulations restricting food advertising aimed at children, reduction in television viewing is a promising approach to reducing excess energy intake. Although a threshold of safe exposure to television and food marketing has not been empirically demonstrated, the American Academy of Pediatrics has long advocated limiting children to no more than 2 hours of television per day to decrease sedentary time and to decrease exposure to content that may encourage a range of negative behaviors.

Jean L. Wiecha et al.,
"When Children Eat What They Watch,"
Archives of Pediatrics & Adolescent Medicine, *April 2006.*

---

sort of marketing policy, only 24 percent of restaurants and 22 percent of entertainment companies have any policy guiding advertising to children.

In a study released in March 2007, the Henry J. Kaiser Family Foundation noted that children ages 2 to 7 see an average of 12 televised food ads a day, or 4,400 a year, and children 8 to 12 see an average of 21 a day—more than 7,600 a year. For teenagers, the numbers are 17 a day, or more than 6,000 a year. Fully half of all ad time on children's shows is for food, the foundation reported.

"Most of the food ads that children and teens see on TV are for foods that nutritionists, watchdog groups and government agencies argue should be consumed either in moderation, occasionally or in small portions," the group found. "Of the 8,854 food ads reviewed in the study, there were no ads for fruits or vegetables targeted at children or teens."

In case you are wondering, several studies have demonstrated that television ads do indeed have an effect—and not a good effect—on what children eat, and how much. In one study of 548 students at five public schools near Boston, published in 2006 in the *Archives of Pediatrics & Adolescent Medicine*, researchers found that for each additional hour of television viewing, the children consumed an additional 167 calories, especially the calorie-dense, low-nutrient foods frequently advertised on television.

Product Placement in Children's Movies

Now, a new study suggests, it's time to attend to more subtle promotions of questionable foods, beverages and eating establishments that appear in movies popular among children and adolescents. "Movies," the authors stated, "are a potent source of advertising to children, which has been largely overlooked."

The study, published in March in the journal *Pediatrics*, analyzed brand placements for foods, beverages and eateries depicted in the top 20 box-office hits for each year from 1996 to 2005. Of the 138 movies analyzed, 49 percent were rated PG-13, 20.5 percent were PG and 7.5 percent were G.

"We found that a surprising proportion of movies that were targeted to children and adolescents featured brand appearances," the authors wrote. Although Coca-Cola and Pepsi have long-standing commitments not to advertise their products on children's television, the researchers found that "sugar-sweetened beverage products from these companies regularly appeared in movies, especially those rated for children and adolescents."

Of the 1,180 brand placements identified, 26 percent of the food placements were for candy and other confections and 21 percent for salty snacks; 76 percent of the beverages were sugar-sweetened drinks, and two-thirds of the restaurants were fast-food places. The researchers found that "soft drinks, chips and fast-food brands dominated PG-rated and PG-13-rated movies."

The authors, led by Lisa A. Sutherland of Dartmouth Medical [School], found an average of 8.6 brand placements per movie, and concluded that most were "for energy-dense, nutrient-poor foods or product lines."

An Insidious Effect

Lest you doubt these brand placements influence young eating habits, the appearance of Reese's Pieces in the movie *E.T.: The Extra-Terrestrial* resulted in a sharp increase in sales in the three months after the movie's release in 1982.

"Movie product placement is on par with subliminal advertising, yet it has been largely ignored by those who study the impact of marketing on children," the authors wrote.

The authors expressed particular concern about the influence of brand placements in movies rated PG and PG-13 on older children and teenagers, "who are gaining independence with respect to their food choices." They noted that this "provides a likely avenue by which brand loyalty and product preference can be built."

What can you do? I wouldn't dare suggest passing up a wonderful movie like *E.T.* But just as parents and others have objected to sugary drinks sold in schools and, to a lesser effect so far, to foods advertised on children's television, it may be time to make your feelings known to movie producers about how brand placements are harming the health and increasing the weight of America's children.

| *"Food and beverage advertising dollars targeting children are down, not up."*

Marketing Food to Children Cannot Be Blamed for Non-Nutritious Food Choices

Paul Kurnit

In the following viewpoint, Paul Kurnit, a professor of marketing at Pace University's Lubin School of Business, claims that advertising cannot be blamed for childhood obesity and poor food choices. He claims that foods and related advertising have been a part of American society for more than fifty years and the practices are basically unchanged. Advertising targeting children is down, not up. Food companies have changed their products to promote healthy living, yet childhood obesity in America is still a large problem. Kurnit believes the solution to be a combination of efforts by parents, teachers, government, industry, and children to inspire social change.

As you read, consider the following questions:

1. In what year did "advocacy groups and politicians" sound "the alarm that America was fat and getting fatter"?

Paul Kurnit, "The Advertising Diet: Why Ads Aren't to Blame for America's Obesity Problems," *AdWeek*, December 3, 2007. Reproduced by permission.

2. What are some reasons given in the viewpoint for the obesity problem in America?

3. How did food companies respond to the blame for causing childhood obesity and poor food choices?

The obesity epidemic in America started five years ago. The ever-widening problem had been building for some time before that, but in 2003, advocacy groups and politicians sounded the alarm that America was fat and getting fatter. Childhood obesity carries with it staggering risks of disease and huge additional costs for medical care.

The obesity outcry of a few years ago was squarely pointed at the food and advertising industries. The simple and pervasive problem, it was claimed, was that food companies were making bad-for-us foods and advertising was causing obesity. If only the problem was that simple, there could likely be a simple solution. But, alas, it just wasn't, it just isn't, the case. In fact, more than 80 percent of parents believe that if their kids are overweight, they are to blame.

Advertising Dollars Targeting Children Are Down

The major food companies, at first, were caught completely off guard by the criticism. Their initial response was "what did we do wrong?" The foods and related advertising promoting them have been part of the American diet for well over 50 years. Baby boomers grew up with presweetened cereal and fast food. Product development and advertising practice have essentially gone unchanged. There are more products and choices, to be sure. The media marketplace has also changed dramatically. But, food and beverage advertising dollars targeting children are down, not up.

The obesity problem is certainly real, though. It is a complex multidimensional issue. The commitment to and budgets for physical education in schools are way down. After-school sports programs have been cut. No one knows what a portion size should be. The food pyramid went from outdated to an update that is so confusing we don't know what an appropriate eating regimen is. Today's parents are afraid to send their kids outside after school to run around. Many moms are so busy they don't have or make the time to cook complete, well-balanced meals for dinner. Everybody's running to the next activity, but too few of us are running for health and wellness. The solution is energy balance: Burn the calories we consume. We are surely out of balance, but food and beverage advertising has nothing to do with that.

The Institute of Medicine 2006 report "Food Marketing to Children and Youth: Threat or Opportunity?" examined every food study conducted in America and found no linkage between advertising and obesity. Advertising informs children about food and beverage brand options, but it does not proscribe quantity or calorie content kids consume.

Food Companies Change Their Products

That notwithstanding, the food companies and advertising agencies got the wake-up call. Frito-Lay removed trans fats from all of its snack products long before New York Mayor Mike Bloomberg even considered the issue. Parent company PepsiCo created a Smart Spot program and issued a corporate edict that a minimum of 50 percent of the company's new products had to fulfill better-for-you food criteria. General Mills reformulated its cereals to use whole grains and altered advertising guidelines to depict its foods in complete and appropriate meal or snacking contexts. Kraft introduced 100-calorie packs, a new line of South Beach Diet products, stated it would no longer advertise its high-fat or sugar products to children and created a new Sensible Solutions program. McDonald's extended a line of salads and revised its Happy Meals to include a choice of skim milk or Apple Dippers in place of soft drinks and fries. Virtually overnight, McDonald's became the largest purchaser of apples in the United States. Other proactive company initiatives in food and advertising practice are being implemented at a dizzying pace.

The corporate actions by the food companies have been dramatic in their range, scope and speed. In a business where new product introductions and corporate policy can take years to implement, market change and impact have moved at light speed. And still the major food companies are under siege. There is a fundamental distrust that they are committed to doing well by doing good. They are. It's a new age. Self-regulation and a new Children's Food and Beverage Advertising Initiative launched by the Council of Better Business Bureaus are working actively and effectively to encourage and realize new marketing practices in health and wellness.

The solution to the obesity crisis is not simple. It will require a wide range of constituencies to pull together to inspire social change—parents, teachers, government, industry and kids themselves. Industry is doing its part. It can and will do more. But, saber-rattling lawsuits and threatened regulation are not the solution. They polarize parties who need to work together to achieve concerted joint action for positive change.

Advertising Has Not Caused Poor Food Choices

To be sure, advertising is a powerful communications form. And youth are powerful ambassadors for social movements. The pervasive adoption of seat-belt usage in this country happened not because of laws, but because kids urged parents to buckle up. The designated driver is a teen initiative that has tremendously reduced drunken driving among youth. Both were promoted through Advertising Council efforts, but both were adopted and evangelized by youth. Word of mouth, the kid buzz network, is the most powerful form of advertising today.

So it can be, should be and will be for health and wellness. Advertising has not caused the obesity epidemic in America, but it can be a major part of the solution to the problem. We need more, not less advertising messaging to kids about good foods, healthy diet, exercise and energy balance. New proactive advertising to engage and inform our youth about the dynamics of wellness can empower kids to drive a new social movement as the ambassadors for a healthier America.

Periodical Bibliography

The following articles have been selected to supplement the diverse views presented in this chapter.

Courtney Bailey	"Supersizing America: Fatness and Post-9/11 Cultural Anxieties," *Journal of Popular Culture*, June 2010.
Ann Cooper	"The Nightmare of School Lunches," *Progressive*, December 2010–January 2011.
Adam Drewnowski	"Obesity, Diets, and Social Inequalities," *Nutrition Reviews*, May 2009.
Liam Julian	"Why School Lunch Is 'Nasty,'" *Policy Review*, October/November 2010.
Claudia Kalb	"Culture of Corpulence," *Newsweek*, March 14, 2010.
Josh Ozersky	"Should the U.S. Crackdown on Happy Meals?" *Time*, November 10, 2010.
Eric Ravussin	"Fat Chance: New Clues to Why We Gain Weight," *Nutrition Action Healthletter*, December 2010.
Claire Suddath	"School Lunches," *Time*, October 7, 2009.
Debra Viadero	"Childhood Obesity," *Education Week*, July 15, 2009.

CHAPTER 4

What Personal
Nutrition and Dietary
Choices Impact Health?

Chapter Preface

Concerns over global warming have led many scientists to look to human food supply chains to determine the impact of food production on the environment. In doing so, they found the livestock industry to be one of the main sources of carbon dioxide emissions from food production. In a 2009 article in the *CCPA Monitor*, Chris Brazier cites statistics presented by the chair of the Intergovernmental Panel on Climate Change, Dr. Rajendra Pachauri, on the subject. In 2008 Pachauri reported not only that "livestock production accounts for 80% of greenhouse gas emissions from agriculture and 18% of all greenhouse gas emissions from human activities," but also that the amount of land required to produce meat far exceeds that needed to produce fruits, vegetables, and grains. While meat consumption is still greater today than it was forty years ago, arguments like these, combined with more traditional reasons such as concern for animal welfare, religious beliefs, and health benefits, have led many individuals to become vegetarians or vegans. Regardless of the reason for doing so, giving up meat, and in the case of veganism, giving up all animal products entirely, is a major choice that can have a significant impact on one's nutritional health.

In October 2009 the *Harvard Women's Health Watch* published an article examining the health benefits of vegetarianism and dietary considerations one must heed to ensure this lifestyle choice remains a healthy and nutritious one. The article notes that while previously the debate about vegetarian diets focused on "potential nutritional deficiencies," current studies have corroborated the view that these diets may contribute to a decreased risk for heart disease, cancer, and type 2 diabetes; however, more research needs to be conducted in order to determine if the decreased risk is a direct result of the dietary choice. The article further confirms that most vegetarians and vegans consume sufficient amounts of necessary nutrients traditionally thought to be lacking in meatless diets, such as calcium, protein, vitamin B12, iron, zinc, and omega-3 fatty acids. Still, the article cautions that appropriate planning is necessary to ensure that a vegetarian diet provides all the expected health benefits.

Planning nutritional intake in one's diet—whether it be vegetarian, vegan, supplement enhanced, gluten free, low in high-fructose corn syrup, or any of the other myriad options available today with the abundance of food choices accessible to the American consumer—is closely tied to an individual's health. As the choices available to consumers increase alongside the coming and going of fad diets and the proliferation of information and misinformation, nutritional choices will become increasingly significant. Each of the viewpoints in the following chapter presents a perspective on specific choices that, according to the respective authors, could improve or injure one's health.

> "Cutting back on high amounts of gluten in wheat products—especially in refined, processed foods—is pretty sound advice for an optimal diet, in general."

Gluten-Free Diets Are Good for Everyone's Health

Sharon Palmer

Many people have sensitivity to gluten, a protein contained in grains such as wheat, rye, and barley. Because of this, there has been an explosion of gluten-free products on the market and available in grocery stores. In the viewpoint that follows, Sharon Palmer argues that these gluten-free options, while a necessity for those who have intolerance to the substance, can be beneficial for anyone's health. Palmer cites Shelley Case, a nutrition expert specializing in gluten-free diets, who touts the benefits of this lifestyle. Still, both are skeptical of going gluten free by simply purchasing the newest products on the market, as these can often contain many unhealthy ingredients even though the gluten has been cut. Sharon Palmer is a registered dietician and the editor of the journal Environmental Nutrition.

Sharon Palmer, "Is the Gluten-Free Diet the Next 'It' Diet for Health?" *Environmental Nutrition*, v. 33, no. 2, February 2010, p. 2. Copyright © 2010 by Belvoir Media Group, LLC. All rights reserved. Reproduced by permission.

As you read, consider the following questions:

1. As Palmer states, by how much did the market for gluten-free products increase from 2004 to 2008?

2. What disease is defined by gluten intolerance, and how many people does it affect, according to Palmer?

3. What is the makeup of the "model of health," gluten-free diet that the author suggests?

"I suggest avoiding gluten," is the advice given by Mark Sisson, author of *The Primal Blueprint*, on his popular health and nutrition blog, *Mark's Daily Apple*. Sisson believes that gluten intolerance is more common than we realize; his theory is that gluten and grains have been introduced relatively recently into the human diet, so it's a smart idea to drop them altogether. Such belief in the benefits of gluten avoidance is not rare. Elisabeth Hasselbeck, co-host of the television show, *The View*, and author of *The G-Free Diet*, purports that a gluten-free diet can increase energy, lower cholesterol, help you lose weight and restore health. A growing number of people are placing gluten, the protein found in wheat, rye, barley and triticale, on their "no" list, in much the same fashion as they once banned fat and carbohydrates.

"It's definitely a hot trend for people to go off gluten. It's like the latest Atkins diet [the low or no carbohydrate weight-loss diet that became popular in the early 2000s]," says Shelley Case, R.D., gluten-free nutrition expert and author of *Gluten-Free Diet, A Comprehensive Resource Guide*. Case reports that the gluten-free-products market increased from $560 million in annual sales in 2004 to $1.56 billion in 2008, and is expected to climb to $26 billion in 2012. That explains why more gluten-free products are filling supermarket shelves. And there wouldn't be a surge in products without the demand.

Fundamentals of the Gluten-Free Diet

Grains that should be avoided
Wheat (includes spelt, kamut, semolina, triticale), rye, barley
(including malt)
Safe grains (gluten-free)
Rice, amaranth, buckwheat, corn, millet, quinoa, sorghum, teff
(an Ethiopian cereal grain), oats
**Sources of gluten-free starches that can be used as flour
alternatives**
Cereal grains: amaranth, buckwheat, corn (polenta), millet, quinoa,
sorghum, teff, rice (white, brown, wild, basmati, jasmine),
montina (Indian rice grass)
Tubers: arrowroot, jicama, taro, potato, tapioca (cassava, manioc,
yucca)
Legumes: chickpeas, lentils, kidney beans, navy beans, pea beans,
peanuts, soybeans
Nuts: almonds, walnuts, chestnuts, hazelnuts, cashews
Seeds: sunflower, flax, pumpkin

TAKEN FROM: *New England Journal of Medicine*, October 25,
2007.

Some Diseases Necessitate
a Gluten-Free Diet

Going completely gluten free is a dire necessity for people diagnosed with celiac disease (CD), a lifelong, digestive disorder affecting both children and adults. When people with CD eat gluten-containing foods, it creates a toxic reaction from the immune system that causes damage to the small intestine and does not allow food to be absorbed properly. Even small amounts of gluten can affect people with CD. Damage can occur to the small bowel even when there are no gastrointestinal symptoms present. CD affects one out of 100 people, making it "the most underdiagnosed disease in America," Case says. A

Mayo Clinic study published in July 2009 in the journal *Gastroenterology* revealed that CD is at least four times more common now than it was 50 years ago. Though researchers don't understand why rates of CD are climbing, some postulate that it might be related to our increasing reliance on high intakes of gluten and wheat. Other gluten-free followers are those with non-celiac gluten sensitivity (an intolerance to gluten that manifests with symptoms such as bloating, abdominal pain and diarrhea) and people with a wheat allergy that must avoid gluten-containing wheat products.

A Gluten-Free Diet Can Benefit Anyone

Case notes that there is little scientific support to back the claims that humans in general should eliminate gluten, but she concedes that we are eating gluten at unprecedented levels. "We are eating a lot of gluten in processed foods and things like bagels, muffins and snack foods. We're carbaholics. We don't eat the same way our grandparents did—they ate smaller amounts of gluten, and primarily in the form of bread," says Case. Cutting back on high amounts of gluten in wheat products—especially in refined, processed foods—is pretty sound advice for an optimal diet, in general.

While the benefits from cutting back on a gluten overload seem obvious, the notion that gluten free equals healthy is a mistake. "People think gluten free is healthier, and it's not so," says Case. "Many people gain weight because gluten-free products mostly contain starches, sugars and fats, and the majority of gluten-free foods are not enriched with vitamins and minerals as wheat products are. People tend to feel deprived when they're on a gluten-free diet, so they often eat more gluten-free baked products, like cookies."

On the other hand, a gluten-free diet can be a model of health with just a little effort. By forging a diet around lean proteins, low-fat dairy products, legumes, nuts, fruits, vegetables and ancient gluten-free whole grains like quinoa, it can be done.

| "There's nothing inherently low calorie
or healthy about a gluten-free diet."

Gluten-Free Diets Are Necessary Only for Those with Gluten Intolerance

Ayala Laufer-Cahana

With the increasing prevalence of gluten-free products on the market, media discussion of gluten-free diets, and the number of people adhering to this type of lifestyle, many have begun to question the touted benefits of gluten-free living for people who do not suffer from gluten intolerance. In the viewpoint that follows, Dr. Ayala Laufer-Cahana argues that there is currently no evidence proving that a gluten-free diet benefits a person without a gluten-related disease, and much of the current interest in the diet is based on hype or anecdotal evidence. While praising the increased awareness of gluten sensitivity and the necessity for some people to cut the protein found in grains from their diets, Laufer-Cahana remains skeptical of the additional benefits attached to gluten-free eating. Ayala Laufer-Cahana is a physician specializing in pediatrics and medical genetics, and she is cofounder of the company Herbal Water.

Ayala Laufer-Cahana, "The Gluten-Free Health Fad: The Good and the Bad—Part 1," Open Salon, May 18, 2009. Copyright © 2009 by Ayala Laufer-Cahana. All rights reserved. Reproduced by permission. http://open.salon.com

As you read, consider the following questions:

1. According to research cited by the author, by how much are gluten-free product sales expected to grow in coming years?

2. As stated by the author, what are the only two "established medical reasons" for cutting gluten from one's diet?

3. What are the two conditions that the author contends are not proven to be affected by a gluten-free diet?

Have you noticed the gluten-free food explosion? I have the privilege of attending many food shows, and I'm stunned by the proliferation of grain-based foods—prepared meals, cookies, snacks bread and crackers—developed for the benefit of those on a gluten-free diet and with "gluten-free" as a marketing proposition.

Gluten-free foods are a necessity for people with celiac disease, a disorder resulting from an immune reaction to gluten. But are these foods good for everyone else?

The Gluten-Free Fad

While the precise prevalence of celiac disease isn't known, it's estimated to range from about 0.4 percent to about one percent of the general population in the U.S. (up to three million Americans). The number of Americans with *physician-diagnosed celiac* however, although growing, is still not very large, and estimated anywhere in the range of 40,000–110,000 cases.

Not to sound cynical, but even a one percent consumer base wouldn't drive manufacturers and retailers to the accelerated expansion of the gluten-free options we're seeing. The reason food manufacturers have jumped full force into this market is because gluten-free products are now favored not only by celiac patients, but by many people *without* the diagnosis—gluten free is indeed the latest food fad—and it's a huge opportunity to make money. Research firm Mintel estimates that nearly 10 percent of shoppers currently seek gluten-free foods; they forecast 15–25 percent growth in gluten-free product sales in coming years.

I'm glad to see the growing awareness of celiac, and also happy to see that keeping a gluten-free diet is becoming easier, more acceptable, and requires less sacrifice on taste.

On the other hand, the "fad" aspect of the gluten-free boom worries me quite a bit.

Only Some People Must Eat Gluten-Free Products

Gluten is a protein found in wheat or related grains. It's a remarkably large molecule that's quite central to the structure and texture of dough.

Gluten is definitely not an evil food component for those not afflicted by celiac. Gluten is part of whole wheat flours and whole wheat, barley and rye grains—parts of a healthy diet. Although many junk foods contain gluten, gluten isn't what makes these foods not nutritious—it's the other ingredients or the processing of the grains that makes them so. If going gluten free means choosing from the gluten-free menu at Wendy's or Dairy Queen, or replacing wheat-based snacks with corn-based ones, you haven't done yourself much good.

There are only two established medical reasons to avoid gluten: celiac disease and dermatitis herpetiformis, a very itchy chronic skin rash of bumps and blisters, frequently linked to celiac. In celiac disease, complete removal of gluten from the diet is necessary for life, and results in complete resolution of symptoms. Non-adherence to a gluten-free diet can have dire consequences (even if the person is asymptomatic), including poor growth, infertility, osteoporosis, anemia, bowel narrowing and bowel cancer.

The Science of Celiac Disease

Gluten . . . has a peculiar structure: It is unusually rich in the amino acids glutamine and proline. This property renders part of the molecule impervious to our protein-chopping machinery, leaving small protein fragments, or peptides, intact. Even so, in healthy people, most of these peptides are kept within the gastrointestinal tract and are simply excreted before the immune system even notices them. And any gluten that sneaks across the gastrointestinal lining is usually too minimal to excite a significant response from a normally functioning immune system.

CD [celiac disease] patients, on the other hand, have inherited a mix of genes that contribute to a heightened immune sensitivity to gluten. . . . Ninety-five percent of people with CD possess the gene either for HLA-DQ2 or for HLA-DQ8, whereas just 30 to 40 percent of the general population have one of those versions. This finding and others suggest that the HLA-DQ2 and HLA-DQ8 genes are not the sole cause of immune hyperactivity but that the disease, nonetheless, is nearly impossible to establish without one of them.

Alessio Fasano,
"Surprises from Celiac Disease,"
Scientific American, *August 2009.*

A gluten-free diet is now touted for many other conditions, from autism to attention deficit disorder, irritated bowel syndrome, multiple sclerosis and now even weight loss.

Although there are *anecdotal* stories about gluten-free diets making a difference for these conditions, there's really no good evidence to support such advice.

Gluten-Free Diet for Autism and Weight Loss Is Unproven

The gluten-free casein (milk protein)-free diet is a very common treatment attempt for autism.

A Cochrane review did an extensive literature search to identify randomized controlled studies of gluten-free or casein-free diets as an intervention in autistic features. They found only two small randomized controlled studies, with a total of 35 patients between them. The results of one of these studies indicated that a combined gluten- and casein-free diet reduced autistic behavior, but the second study showed no significant difference in outcome measures between the diet group and the control group.

The researchers concluded (emphasis is mine):

> "Research has shown high rates of use of complementary and alternative therapies (CAM) for children with autism including gluten and/or casein exclusion diets. **Current evidence for efficacy of these diets is poor**. Large scale, good quality randomised controlled trials are needed."

There's no logical reason why adopting a gluten-free regimen should result in weight loss. Unless you have a strategy of reducing caloric intake on what just happens to be a gluten-free regimen, I can't see how gluten free for weight reduction makes any sense.

In fact, patients with celiac often *gain* weight once they start a gluten-free regimen. The reason is that while they're eating gluten, many suffer abdominal pain, malabsorption and other symptoms that lead to reduced consumption or utilization of food. Once they're on the gluten-free diet they thrive, eat well and gain weight.

Perhaps paying more attention to food—no matter what the regimen—can *anecdotally* lead to weight loss, but *there's nothing inherently low calorie or healthy about a gluten-free diet.*

Gluten-Free Diet Hype

I learned from nutritionist Janet Helm about [*The View* television show host] Elisabeth Hasselbeck's book *The G-Free Diet*, which Janet criticizes for inaccuracies, and also for "glorifying gluten-free and making it appear to be the best thing since, um, sliced bread."

In the introduction to her book, Hasselbeck (who has celiac disease, and therefore greatly benefited from going gluten free) writes:

> "But a gluten-free lifestyle can help countless others as well. People suffering from a wide range of diseases—from autism to osteoporosis, from diabetes to rheumatoid arthritis—can often benefit from this change in diet. Even people with no health issues have a great deal to gain by giving up gluten. The G-free diet can help with weight management. It can elevate your energy levels, improve your attention span, and speed up your digestion."

To which all I have to say is: Show us the proof! I searched Medline (the online computer database for biomedical journals) and couldn't find it.

| "Our government's nutrient guidelines ignore the fact that many Americans, because of genetic variations and unique needs, may need higher doses of vitamins and minerals than the [Recommended Dietary Allowance]."

Dietary Supplements Can Improve One's Health

Mark Hyman

The term nutritional supplement encompasses a wide range of products taken to complement an individual's regular diet and provide additional nutrients. While some health care professionals maintain that people can get all the necessary nutrients by eating a healthy, balanced diet, others champion a dietary program that includes a variety of nutritional supplements. Mark Hyman is one of these professionals, and in the following viewpoint, he argues that nutritional supplements provide not only health benefits but also economic benefits in the form of health care savings. Hyman cites research that shows the positive impact of taking nutritional supplements on specific health conditions. In addition, he contends that beyond health conditions, Americans currently do not receive the needed nutrients from

Mark Hyman, "How Dietary Supplements Reduce Health Care Costs," *Huffington Post*, July 10, 2010. Content by Mark Hyman © 2010. Used with permission.

their food, and thus should be taking supplements to round out their normal diets. Mark Hyman is a family physician who developed the Functional Medicine approach, which emphasizes treatment of the whole patient, not just the cause of illness.

As you read, consider the following questions:

1. What four conditions and corresponding nutritional therapies does Hyman cite from the Lewin Group study as being "unquestionable, beyond scientific doubt"?

2. As stated by the author, what are the combined savings over a five-year period that could be generated by complying with the four supplemental interventions recommended by the Lewin study?

3. According to Hyman, what percentage of Americans is deficient in one or more nutrients when compared to the Recommended Dietary Allowance level?

New research from the Lewin Group [an organization that provides research and consulting services for the healthcare industry] has shown that spending pennies a day on a few key nutritional supplements can dramatically reduce sickness and chronic disease—and greatly decrease healthcare expenditures as a result. How did they come to this conclusion? And why haven't we heard about it?

The Lewin Group looked only at rigorous scientific studies that documented the benefits of nutritional supplements. They used the Congressional Budget Office's accounting methods to determine the economic impact of supplements. And they kept their analysis specifically to Medicare patients and women of childbearing age. . . .

The Unquestionable Benefits of Certain Nutritional Therapies

Although nutritional therapies can help a broad range of illnesses, the group only looked at four supplements and disease combinations because of the rigor and validity of the scientific evidence available for these nutrients and diseases.

While there are many other beneficial nutritional therapies that have been proven helpful in studies, the ones in this particular study are only those that are unquestionable, beyond scientific doubt, well-accepted, and proven to help. Yet they are also underused and not generally recommended by healthcare providers. The study looked at:

1. Calcium and vitamin D and their effect on osteoporosis

2. Folic acid and its ability to prevent birth defects

3. Omega-3 fatty acids and their benefits for heart disease

4. Lutein and zeaxanthin and their benefit in preventing major age-related blindness, or macular degeneration

In this study, the researchers were extremely strict and only looked at nutrient interventions that met three criteria.

1. The supplement had to produce a measurable physiological effect.

2. This physiological effect had to create a change in health status.

3. The researchers only looked at health problems where a change in health status is associated with a decrease in healthcare expenditures.

Now, most of us hear the refrain from our physicians that nutritional supplements just produce expensive urine, that you do not know what you are getting, or that there is no scientific proof to support their claims. Based on this study and many others like it, my advice to these doctors is to do their scientific homework. Let's start by looking at the effects of calcium and vitamin D.

Supplements Provide Health and Economic Benefits

First, I want to point out the vitamin D research referred to in the Lewin Group study is older research. Newer research . . . suggests that higher doses of vitamin D3, such as 1,000 to 2,000 IU [international unit, which measures the effect of a substance] a day, have even greater benefit.

Yet even by focusing only on the older research, this study's authors determined that providing Medicare-age citizens with 1,200 mg [milligrams] of calcium and 400 IU of vitamin D would result in reduced bone loss and fewer hip fractures. The researchers estimated these supplements could prevent more than 776,000 hospitalizations for hip fractures over five years and save $16.1 billion.

Next let's look at omega-3 fats. Omega-3 fatty acids help prevent cardiac arrhythmias, improve cell membrane function, reduce inflammation, lower cholesterol and blood pressure, and have many other benefits.

The Lewin Group found that giving the Medicare population about 1,800 mg of omega-3 fats a day would prevent 374,000 hospitalizations from heart disease over five years. The Medicare savings from reduced hospital and physician expenses would be $3.2 billion.

This is pretty convincing data, but it doesn't stop there. The Lewin Group also analyzed the economic effects of lutein and zeaxanthin—carotenoids that are found in yellow and orange vegetables. I recommend taking them in combination with the hundreds of other carotenoids found in yellow and orange foods.

Taken as supplements, these have been shown to treat macular degeneration, which is the loss of central vision, a major reason people over age 65 require nursing home care. The study found that taking 6 to 10 mg of lutein and zeaxanthin daily would help 190,000 individuals avoid dependent care and would result in $3.6 billion in savings over five years.

Lastly the Lewin Group looked at the effects of taking folic acid. 44 million women of childbearing age are not taking folic acid. If only 11.3 million of them began taking just 400 mcg [microgram] of folic acid on a daily basis before conception, we could prevent birth defects called neural tube defects in 600 babies and save $344,700,000 in lifetime healthcare costs for these children. Over 5 years, this would account for $1.4 billion in savings.

Taken together, these four simple interventions, which cost pennies a day, could produce a combined savings of $24 billion over five years. This does not even include benefits to people younger than 65 or any of the other benefits of nutritional supplementation, such as improved immunity, cognitive function, and mood.

Supplements Are Necessary for a Complete Diet

The Lewin Group's study is intriguing. The economic impact of investing a few pennies a day in nutritional supplements is compelling. But what's downright frightening is that studies by the US Department of Health and Human Services prove that the typical American diet does not always provide a sufficient level of vitamins and minerals—meaning we are at greater risk for conditions like those outlined above.

Because of our consumption of low-nutrient, high-calorie foods that are highly processed, hybridized, genetically modified, shipped long distances, and grown in nutrient-depleted soils, many of us are nutritionally depleted.

In fact, a whopping 92 percent of us are deficient in one or more nutrients at the Recommended [Dietary] Allowance (RDA) level, which is the minimum amount necessary to prevent deficiency diseases like rickets or scurvy—diseases that are the result of not getting enough vitamins and minerals. The RDA standards do not necessarily outline the amount needed for optimal health.

The Definition of a Dietary Supplement

Dietary supplements were defined in 1994 by Congress under the Dietary Supplement Health and Education Act (DSHEA). Under DSHEA, a product is a dietary supplement if it does the following:

1. Intended to supplement the diet

2. Contains dietary ingredients, such as vitamins, minerals, herbs (other than tobacco), amino acids, other natural substances, and/or their constituents

3. Ingested orally in the form of a pill, capsule, tablet, or liquid

4. Labeled on the front panel of the product as a dietary supplement

5. Sold and marketed as a dietary ingredient before October 15, 1994, or has been approved by the United States Food and Drug Administration (FDA) as a new dietary ingredient (NDI)

6. Intended use is as a dietary supplement, not as a food or a drug.

Jacqueline Jacques, "The Professional's Guide to Nutritional Supplements: Understanding Quality and Regulatory Issues," Bariatric Times, vol. 7, no. 10, October 2010.

What's more, our government's nutrient guidelines ignore the fact that many Americans, because of genetic variations and unique needs, may need higher doses of vitamins and minerals than the RDA. Vitamin deficiency does not cause acute diseases such as scurvy or rickets, but they do cause what have been called "long-latency deficiency diseases." These include conditions like blindness, osteoporosis, heart disease, cancer, diabetes, dementia, and more.

What all this adds up to is clear. Nutritional supplements do not just make expensive urine. Based on mounting evidence and confirmed by the *JAMA: Journal of the American Medical Association* and the *New England Journal of Medicine*, I strongly believe that we should all be taking certain basic supplements.

> *"Across the spectrum, most nutrition experts agree that vitamin and mineral pills—even ones that hold tremendous potential and do provide benefits—can actually be harmful too."*

Dietary Supplements Can Be Dangerous to One's Health

Cathy Gulli

While sales of nutritional supplements have exploded in recent years, many within the health field question the benefit of these dietary additions. In the viewpoint that follows, Cathy Gulli maintains that the evidence from numerous studies combined with the experiences of many health professionals has shown that often nutrient supplements can do more harm to an individual's health than good. She cites the opinions of a wide variety of experts from within the medical field, supplement industry, and academia. All in all, Gulli concludes that when dietary supplementation is conducted with the personalized guidance of a health care provider, it can be beneficial to one's health, but since this type of care is not readily available to most people,

Cathy Gulli, "How Vitamins Can Be Hazardous to Your Health," *Maclean's*, vol. 121, no. 15, April 21, 2008. Copyright © 2008 Maclean's Magazine. All rights reserved. Reproduced by permission.

adding nutrient supplements to one's diet remains a risky proposition. Cathy Gulli is an associate editor for the weekly Canadian magazine Maclean's.

As you read, consider the following questions:

1. As cited by Gulli, what were the findings of the United Kingdom's Food Standards Agency study on thirty-four vitamins and minerals?

2. What are some of the unfounded supplement fads mentioned by the author as being popular in the 1970s, 80s, and 90s?

3. According to Health Canada and the University of California, Berkeley *Wellness Letter* cited by Gulli, what are some of the health condition–supplement combinations that can cause dangerous side effects?

Convention says calcium is good for bones. But if you read recent research you might never take calcium supplements again. They may increase the risk of heart attack in healthy postmenopausal women, according to a report by scientists at the University of Auckland in January's *British Medical Journal*. Incidentally, postmenopausal women are probably the group mostly taking calcium pills to prevent osteoporosis, which makes bones more breakable. Then, in March, the *Harvard Health Letter* announced that "high calcium may not prevent fractures." Confused?

Consumers aren't the only ones. Turns out the incessant flow of contradictory studies released daily is stumping just about everybody, says Gerry Harrington of the Ottawa-based Nonprescription Drug Manufacturers Association, whose members include vitamin and mineral supplement makers. "Health Canada struggles with it. Manufacturers struggle with it. There are even individual scientists who struggle," he concedes. Harrington's warning: "Pay attention. Don't take anything for granted."

Across the spectrum, most nutrition experts agree that vitamin and mineral pills—even ones that hold tremendous potential and do provide benefits—can actually be harmful too. Most damage happens when they're consumed in excess—at doses 10 or more times higher than the recommended daily intake. Even multivitamins can contain very high doses of certain nutrients, as vitamins and minerals are collectively known. Nutrient supplements "can have very negative human consequences" if mishandled, says Bill Jeffery of the Centre for Science in the Public Interest in Ottawa.

Nutrient Supplements Can Have Harmful Effects

The evidence is mounting: In January, the Mayo Clinic declared that certain nutrient pills such as beta-carotene and vitamin E either had no effect or appeared to increase cancer incidence and mortality. The U.S. National Institutes of Health, in a 2006 study, concluded in part that the safety and quality of multivitamin and mineral supplements are inadequate, and uncovered "disturbing evidence of risk" associated with taking some nutrient supplements. And back in 2003, the U.K.'s [United Kingdom's] Food Standards Agency studied 34 vitamins and minerals and found that one could cause cancer, six could induce "irreversible, harmful effects," and three could have "short-term harmful effects." . . .

Taking too many or too much of just one [supplement], such as vitamin C, can lead to an overdose that causes diarrhea; in more serious cases, excess vitamin A can induce liver damage. Moreover, some nutrients such as E and K shouldn't be taken in combination with particular medications, including the widely prescribed blood thinner warfarin. Even a history of smoking or kidney disease can put people at more risk for illness or death if they take some vitamins or minerals. Many people don't even talk with their doctor about the nutrients they're taking. Instead they self-prescribe. And then they miss the latest study that contradicts the one that got them started on vitamin supplements in the first place.

Of course, when a person suffers a real deficiency of vitamins or minerals, the use of supplements can produce remarkable results, says Susan Whiting, a member of Dietitians of Canada, and professor and head of nutrition at the University of Saskatchewan. It's universally agreed upon that pregnant women should consume folic acid to prevent birth defects such as spina bifida. And in sun-deprived locations such as Canada in the winter, the case for vitamin D supplementation seems to make sense. Some people in the health care community even declare the use of vitamins and minerals at high doses as the future of personalized medicine, which will see supplements used as drugs in a targeted way.

The reality, however, is that for many people, deciding what vitamin or mineral pill to take is a relatively arbitrary process. Supplements, says Harrington, come in and out of fashion regularly. And some of the public, adds Jeffery, seems to be "philosophically predisposed to believe that some claims are just true," even when there is little or no scientific proof. Barry Power, an Ottawa pharmacist and director of practice development at the Canadian Pharmacists Association, says that most of us don't see health products that come without a prescription, especially vitamins, as having potentially negative effects. "You can buy them anywhere, they're natural. How harmful can they be?" he quips.

His response is blunt. "Warfarin is natural, it's derived from clover. Aspirin comes from willow bark; if you take enough, you die from it." The bottom line for Power: "Natural does not equate safe."

Unsubstantiated Claims of Supplementation's Healing Power

Over the last century or more, several nutrients have been heralded with their share of fanfare. "There's a long history," says Dr. John Swartzberg, a professor of public health at the University of California, Berkeley. Vitamin C was celebrated for thwarting scurvy and vitamin D was acclaimed as a prevention for rickets. Those discoveries, which held true, gave way to a new chapter in humankind's pursuit of self-preservation—this time, through the power of supplementation. "By taking pills," explains Swartzberg, "we could correct terrible things and save life."

Unfortunately, "that led to all kinds of wild claims," he says. In the 1970s, Nobel Prize–winning chemist Linus Pauling pronounced vitamin C a cure for the common cold; in fact, he took a daily hit of it. But to this day, there's no good proof to corroborate his claim, as a meta-analysis (a study of existing research) by Australian and Finnish researchers showed in 2007. . . .

Come the 1980s and '90s, antioxidants such as vitamin E, C and beta-carotene were all the rage with proclamations that they could prevent cancer, recalls dietitian Whiting. As it turned out, beta-carotene has been shown by Finnish and American researchers to actually increase the incidence of lung cancer among smokers, former smokers, asbestos workers and others at high risk. "What's that about?" Swartzberg, a physician, remembers thinking. Until then, many cardiologists had been recommending beta-carotene to patients; suddenly it all changed. Doctors, caught off guard by new and clashing studies, could only do one thing: "We reneged," says Swartzberg.

To make matters worse, a meta-analysis in the *Annals of Internal Medicine* in 2005 showed that high doses of vitamin E—400 international units (a measure of potency) or more a day—could boost all-cause mortality; that is, excessive E can increase the chance of death. "We don't know if it's a statistical fluke," concedes Swartzberg, who chairs the editorial board of the University of California, Berkeley *Wellness Letter*, an authoritative report on nutrition and prevention news, "or something more serious." But a review by the College of Family Physicians of Canada found the results credible and it recommends doctors counsel patients about the risk of excess E.

Misinformation Makes Appropriate Nutrient Supplementation Difficult

More common than these dramatic shifts, though, is the barrage of conflicting studies about vitamins and minerals—which the average person may not be aware of. In early March, *Harvard Men's Health Watch* warned males that multivitamins and excess folic acid may be linked to cancer and should be avoided. A few weeks later, scientists at the University of California, Berkeley published a study in the journal *Human Reproduction* that found high folic acid intake was linked to healthier sperm. What's a guy to do?

"There's a lot of misinformation out there," says Dr. Dugald Seely, a naturopathic doctor in Toronto and director of research and clinical epidemiology at the Canadian College of Naturopathic Medicine. Nutrient supplements are rarely dangerous, Seely says, but that doesn't mean there's no risk. He is calling for more research into complementary medicine. "It's important to not believe everything you hear," says Seely, who sits on Health Canada's Expert Advisory Committee on the Vigilance of Health Products. . . .

Unsafe Doses of Supplements Cause Health Problems

So what do—or should—we know about the dangers of nutrient pills? There's little data on how many people have gotten sick or died from excess intake generally, and pharmacist Power says it's not extremely common. But taking a multivitamin in combination with other nutrient supplements can lead to an overdose, he explains, and "it can be potentially harmful." This is especially easy with fat-soluble vitamins such as A and E because they accumulate in the body.

FDA Regulation of Supplements Is Lax

Most supplements are consumed without raising safety concerns. Still, the products are much less closely scrutinized than drugs, which are tested extensively and must win FDA [U.S. Food and Drug Administration] approval before going on the market. Supplements that are made from products that were on the U.S. market before 1994—as most commonplace ones are—can be sold without being reviewed by the FDA beforehand. Companies that include newer substances are supposed to inform the agency before they go on the market, but don't have to wait for approval.

*Anna Wilde Mathews,
"What's Really in Supplements?—Regulators and
Physicians Raise Alarms About Dangerous
Ingredients in Many Herbal Remedies,"
Wall Street Journal, September 8, 2009.*

Excess C may cause burning urination, adds Power, or diarrhea. "Too much vitamin C can change the colour of your skin," says Jeffery of the Centre for Science in the Public Interest, making it orangey. It may even interfere with your body's ability to metabolize iron and contribute to kidney stones. Excess magnesium can cause diarrhea as well. So can iron, plus constipation and vomiting. Too much vitamin E can cause blurred vision, headaches, dizziness and, of course, diarrhea. Sound bad?

There's worse. Excess zinc may impair blood cell formation, depress the immune system and reduce "good" cholesterol levels, not to mention interfere with copper absorption. (It also can upset your stomach.) B6 can induce nerve damage if overconsumed. And too much vitamin A can cause liver damage and birth defects, besides headaches, scaly skin and hair loss.

Despite the danger, we overconsume nutrient pills because of a "some-is-good-so-more-is-better" mentality that experts say is pervasive throughout North America. Since 1997, Health Canada and the Institute of Medicine have defined "upper tolerable levels" for most vitamins and minerals, which indicate the maximum amount that can be consumed with no adverse effect. But those don't usually appear on labels, and most people aren't aware they even exist.

Also unknown to many consumers are the bad combinations of nutrient supplements and prescription medications. "Vitamin E," says Power, "has interactions with blood thinners such as warfarin. It can increase the anticoagulant effect so you're more prone to bleeding." And calcium, he says, can prevent the body from absorbing antibiotics, including commonly prescribed ones such as ciprofloxacin (Cipro) and tetracycline.

Even people who aren't on doctor-prescribed drugs but have a particular medical history can run into trouble when they take nutrient supplements. According to Health Canada and the Berkeley *Wellness Letter*, if you have kidney disease, magnesium isn't for you. Selenium's not great for people who have had nonmelanoma skin cancer, and niacin should be avoided if you have diabetes, gout, peptic ulcers, liver disease or glaucoma. And people who have hemochromatosis, a hereditary disorder that causes them to absorb too much iron, should not take more of it or they may suffer sexual dysfunction, joint pain, headaches and diabetes.

Professional Consultation Is Necessary for Healthy Supplementation

One of the most risky aspects of vitamin and mineral supplementation is that some people are indifferent or don't believe that it's important to talk to their medical doctor about natural health products before taking them, according to a 2005 Ipsos Reid survey for Health Canada. Dr. Larry Reynolds, a Winnipeg family physician and professor at the University of Manitoba, says that physicians tend to be suspicious or dismissive of alternative health models, and supplement use can trigger a conflict between them and their patients. "There are many people who are understandably afraid of doctors," he says, "We can be scary, and the diagnosis can be scary."

Instead, people self-prescribe based on print media (76 per cent) or info from friends, family and colleagues (66 per cent), revealed a survey by the Canadian Council of Food and Nutrition. That's scary because serious conditions may go unattended for too long, says Reynolds, though he acknowledges patients' desire to feel independent. "They say, I'm losing weight and I have rectal bleeding, so I'll take extra iron," because they think it's an indigestion problem, he explains. "But we want to make sure that it's not cancer of the stomach or bowel. That's why it's important that we work together."

At Scienta Health, a private medical clinic in Toronto, the use of vitamin and mineral supplements is an essential part of keeping patients healthy. Its team of physicians, naturopaths, fitness trainers and psychologists practices nutrigenomics, which uses nutrient and food allergy blood tests and a computerized diagnostic model to determine each person's risk for diseases and nutrient deficiencies. That information gets translated into a tailored menu of high-dose, highly bioavailable (very absorbable) vitamin and mineral supplements that are taken for a time, then revaluated and adjusted depending on changing needs.

"Supplements," say Scienta's co-founder and chief medical officer Dr. Elaine Chin, "should be treated as a form of medication, and used in a very targeted, evidence-based way." She believes that the evolution of personalized medicine will be rooted in this kind of preventative approach to health care using supplementary nutrients and lifestyle. Whiting agrees that vitamins and mineral pills can be tremendously beneficial. "If you are low in something, then you are given that nutrient, you'll have a turnaround," she explains. "For every true deficiency, the nutrient has a wondrous effect."

But for most of us, the kind of complex and attentive care offered at Scienta is unknown; three-quarters of us aren't even able to see a physician the same day we need one. And considering the current doctor shortage, many observers don't see nutritional personalized medicine becoming common any time soon. Reynolds says that his preference is to focus on the known needs of patients rather than on this growing area of medicine. "It does hold promise," he says, "but we're not there yet."

Periodical Bibliography

The following articles have been selected to supplement the diverse views presented in this chapter.

Joy Bauer — "Everything You Need to Know About Salt," *Woman's Day*, March 2011.

Consumer Reports on Health — "Are the Top-Selling Vitamins Worth Taking?" March 2011.

Gerald W. Deas — "Don't Become a Meat Head by Eating Too Much Meat," *New York Amsterdam News*, June 4, 2009.

Jennifer Goldstein — "High Fructose Corn Syrup: How Dangerous Is It?" *Prevention*, May 2009.

Alexandra Gross — "Eating Mercury," *E—The Environmental Magazine*, May–June 2009.

Katherine Harmon — "Worts and All," *Scientific American*, August 2010.

Jane Hart — "The Health Benefits of a Vegetarian Diet," *Alternative & Complementary Therapies*, April 2009.

Nanci Hellmich — "Head to Head, Bod to Bod, Who Wins the Diet Contest?" *USA Today*, August 3, 2010.

Bonnie Liebman — "The Real Cost of Red Meat," *Nutrition Action Healthletter*, June 2009.

Roni Caryn Rabin — "Regimens: Eat Your Vegetables, but Not Too Many," *New York Times*, May 24, 2010.

Bob Trebilcock — "If Your Diet Pill Works . . . It's Bad for You," *Prevention*, February 2011.

For Further Discussion

Chapter 1

1. Both Michael Pollan and Rachel Laudan present historical stories and evidence to support their views about modern food production techniques. Pollan uses the example of his mother to show that food consumption used to be focused on taking time to prepare meals in one's home from natural ingredients purchased in the store. Laudan uses historical examples to show that the romanticized idea of food consumption in earlier eras is inaccurate in its view that food was healthier and safer. How does the authors' use of the past influence your agreement or disagreement with their views? Which viewpoint is more convincing? Use quotes from the viewpoints to support your claims.

2. Organic foods have become pervasive in society today with many grocery stores expanding to fill their shelves with organic products in order to compete with a growing number of independent and chain grocers specializing in these products. Reread viewpoints three and four in the first chapter and decide if you believe that organic foods really are more nutritious than conventionally farmed foods. The authors of both viewpoints present scientific studies to support their claims. Do you find the use of these studies in one viewpoint to be stronger than the other? Are their additional considerations that either viewpoint is not taking into account in their assessment of the studies? Respond to specific examples from the viewpoints in your answer.

3. The last viewpoints in Chapter 1 discuss the ongoing problem of hunger in both the United States and the

world. Conduct some outside research into the topics of the first few viewpoints of this chapter: modern food production techniques and organic farming. How do these two methods of food production impact hunger? Does one provide more food than the other? Are both types of production suitable for all countries and all circumstances? Does one method provide a better opportunity to eradicate hunger? Why? Include quotes from your research to support your claims.

Chapter 2

1. Laura Vanderkam argues that the disbursal of food stamps encourages recipients to spend these vouchers unwisely on high-calorie foods that may add to obesity problems in the United States. Michele Ver Ploeg and Katherine Ralston counter that no studies have shown that such spending habits are connected to weight gain. After reading both viewpoints, which do you find more convincing? Why? Explain your answer.

2. Many of the viewpoints in this chapter contend that disincentives (such as taxes) can encourage people to make more nutritious food choices at restaurants and grocery stores. Do you support the argument that government should be influencing personal food choices? What would be the possible benefits? What would be the potential harms? Above all, explain whether you believe taxes and other government strictures would help citizens lead healthier lives.

Chapter 3

1. The viewpoints by the School Nutrition Association and Adam Bornstein debate the issue that school meals are not meeting the nutrition needs of their students and that some schools are using vending machines to offer junk food that undermines the "good health" message. After

reading these two viewpoints and any other articles you can find on the topic, explain whether you think schools are fulfilling the promise to encourage good health or whether schools are sending mixed messages to students that may work against maintaining a healthy lifestyle.

2. In the pair of viewpoints on marketing food to children, the authors debate whether the food industry is acting ethically in promoting high-sugar or empty-calorie foods to young people. Jane E. Brody believes such marketing—including television commercials for junk food—encourages young people to eat foods that could lead to un-needed weight gain. Paul Kurnit, however, insists obesity rates have increased in young people despite changes food companies have made to promote healthy living. Whose argument do you find more persuasive? Explain why.

3. The viewpoints in this chapter attempt to explain what social and cultural factors may account for personal nutritional habits. Make a list of the influences that you think lead to poor nutrition (you may go beyond the potential causes included in the chapter) and rank them from the most to the least harmful. In your list, explain what effect each social or cultural influence has on the individual, and suggest some ways the harmful impacts could be countered or lessened.

Chapter 4

1. Gluten-free diets have become increasingly popular in recent years as celebrities have begun endorsing them and a wide variety of books and products have appeared touting their benefits. Reread the viewpoints that pertain to this topic and decide whether you think gluten-free diets are important only for those who have celiac disease, or if there are benefits for everyone. Then, do some outside research into gluten-free products. Investigate the cost, nutritional information, and availability. Do you think a

gluten-free diet provides a healthy alternative to a diet that includes gluten? Give information from your research and the viewpoints to support your view.

Organizations to Contact

The editors have compiled the following list of organizations concerned with the issues debated in this book. The descriptions are derived from materials provided by the organizations. All have publications or information available for interested readers. The list was compiled on the date of publication of the present volume; the information provided here may change. Be aware that many organizations take several weeks or longer to respond to inquiries, so allow as much time as possible.

Action Against Hunger/ACF International (ACF)
247 W. Thirty-seventh Street, 10th Floor
New York, NY   10018
(212) 967-7800 • fax: (212) 967-5480
e-mail: info@actionagainsthunger.org
website: www.actionagainsthunger.org

An international humanitarian organization, Action Against Hunger/ACF International (ACF) is dedicated to fighting and eradicating world hunger and malnutrition through sustainable solutions, particularly during and in the aftermath of conflict, war, and natural disaster. The organization's main areas of focus include nutrition, food security, water, sanitation, and hygiene. Publications by ACF include "Strategic Programming for Community Nutrition Interventions," "Introduction to Food Security Intervention Principles," and "Acute Malnutrition: A Preventable Pandemic." These publications and others can be downloaded from the ACF website.

Canadian Council of Food and Nutrition (CCFN)
2810 Matheson Boulevard East, 1st Floor
Mississauga, Ontario   L4W 4X7
   Canada
(905) 625-5746
e-mail: info@ccfn.ca
website: www.ccfn.ca

The Canadian Council of Food and Nutrition (CCFN) was mandated by the National Institute of Nutrition in 2004. CCFN is a nonprofit agency dedicated to distributing health information to all Canadians and promoting wellness policies as part of government legislation. The organization's website offers various press releases and consumer fact sheets that provide statistical research on nutritional and general health topics. CCFN also sponsors research papers that tackle health issues such as obesity, vitamin intake, and the consumption of fat and sodium.

Food Research and Action Center (FRAC)
1875 Connecticut Avenue NW, Suite 540
Washington, DC   20009
(202) 986-2200 • fax: (202) 986-2525
website: www.frac.org

The Food Research and Action Center (FRAC) is a nonprofit organization that seeks to put an end to hunger in the United States through the implementation of improved public policies and the creation of public-private partnerships. To achieve this goal, FRAC combines research with advocacy for improved policy, provides training and support for workers on the front lines of the hunger epidemic, and produces information campaigns to improve public awareness of hunger issues. The organization's website contains information about current legislation, FRAC initiatives, and federal food and nutrition programs, as well as work being conducted on a state level. In addition, the FRAC website offers statistics about hunger and food hardship, participation in food stamp programs, and publications detailing federal and state programs aimed at curbing hunger and improving nutritional intake.

Healthy Kids Challenge (HKC)
2 W Road 210, Dighton, KS   67839
(888) 259-6287 • fax: (620) 397-5979
website: www.healthykidschallenge.com

Healthy Kids Challenge (HKC) is a nonprofit organization that works with schools and other community organizations to keep children healthy. HKC promotes good nutrition behaviors and exercise through various programs available on its website. These programs include in-classroom activities as well as family-based activities that can help motivate children to eat nutritionally sound foods and maintain good health.

Organic Center
PO Box 20513, Boulder, CO   80308
(303) 499-1840
website: www.organic-center.org

The Organic Center is an organization whose mission is to spread information about the benefits of organic foods. It disseminates research, works to increase organic production and consumption, and creates partnerships that benefit the mission. The center provides a general definition of organic foods; reports about issues such as antioxidants, food safety, and nutritional quality; and links to resources with additional information about organic foods for consumers, scientists, and leaders.

School Nutrition Association (SNA)
120 Waterfront Street, Suite 300, National Harbor, MD   20745
(301) 686-3100 • fax: (301) 686-3115
e-mail: servicecenter@schoolnutrition.org
website: www.schoolnutrition.org

The School Nutrition Association (SNA) is a national collective of nutritionists and other food service professionals who seek to make nutritious food available to all schoolchildren. The SNA sets guidelines and offers education concerning school meal programs. It publishes *School Nutrition* and the *Journal of Child Nutrition & Management*. The organization's website also features research, reports, and brochures related to nutrition in schools.

US Department of Agriculture (USDA)
1400 Independence Avenue SW, Washington, DC   20250
(202) 720-2791
website: www.usda.gov

The US Department of Agriculture (USDA) is the government agency charged with overseeing agricultural production in the United States. As such, the office seeks to expand and support economic development of agriculture in the United States and abroad, enhance food safety, and improve nutrition and health. The USDA is in charge of the site Nutrition.gov, which provides current information about government nutrition initiatives, the food pyramid, nutrition and health issues, meal planning, and dietary supplements among other topics. The USDA also oversees the government's organic foods program and provides detailed information about the production of organics.

US Food and Drug Administration (FDA)

10903 New Hampshire Avenue, Silver Spring, MD   20993
(888) 463-6332
website: www.fda.gov

The US Food and Drug Administration (FDA) is the government agency that creates and enforces the regulations tied to food and drug safety. Food areas regulated by the FDA include biotechnology, dietary supplements, food ingredients, and packaging (including nutrition labeling). The FDA provides information about all these topics on its website.

Weston A. Price Foundation

PMB 106-380, 4200 Wisconsin Avenue NW
Washington, DC   20016
(202) 363-4394 • fax: (202) 363-4396
e-mail: info@westonaprice.org
website: www.westonaprice.org

The Weston A. Price Foundation is a nonprofit organization dedicated to spreading the ideas and teachings of American dentist Weston A. Price who, spurred by his observations of teeth, researched the dietary intake of individuals living in nonindustrialized societies and argued that the diets followed in these societies provided the ideal nutrients for humans. The foundation's website provides extensive information about nutrition, modern foods, and traditional diets, among other topics. *Wise Traditions in Food, Farming, and the Healing Arts* is the quarterly journal of the organization, featuring articles on topics relating to nutrition and human diets.

World Health Organization (WHO)
Avenue Appia 20, Geneva 27   1211
   Switzerland
+ 41 22 791 21 11 • fax: +41 22 791 31 11
e-mail: info@who.int
website: www.who.int

The World Health Organization (WHO) is an international organization within the United Nations that is responsible for overseeing all health-related initiatives, agendas, and norms and standards, as well as assisting countries in monitoring and assessing health trends. WHO provides general information and statistics about nutrition as well as technical information about how countries can develop positive nutrition intervention programs. Nutrition-related information and publications are available for download from the WHO website.

Bibliography of Books

Linda Bacon
Health at Every Size: The Surprising Truth About Your Weight. Dallas, TX: BenBella, 2008.

Joel Berg
All You Can Eat: How Hungry Is America? New York: Seven Stories Press, 2008.

Kelly D. Brownell and Katherine Battle Horgen
Food Fight: The Inside Story of the Food Industry, America's Obesity Crisis, and What We Can Do About It. New York: McGraw-Hill, 2004.

Cindy Burke
To Buy or Not to Buy Organic: What You Need to Know to Choose the Healthiest, Safest, Most Earth-Friendly Food. New York: Marlowe & Company, 2007.

T. Colin Campbell and Thomas M. Campbell II
The China Study: The Most Comprehensive Study of Nutrition Ever Conducted and the Startling Implications for Diet, Weight Loss and Long-Term Health. Dallas, TX: BenBella, 2005.

Hank Cardello with Doug Garr
Stuffed: An Insider's Look at Who's (Really) Making America Fat. New York: HarperCollins, 2009.

Ann Cooper and Lisa M. Holmes
Lunch Lessons: Changing the Way We Feed Our Children. New York: HarperCollins, 2006.

Glenn A. Gaesser   *Big Fat Lies: The Truth About Your Weight and Your Health.* Carlsbad, CA: Gürze, 2002.

Paul M. Insel et al.   *Nutrition.* 4th ed. Sudbury, MA: Jones and Bartlett, 2011.

Bill Lambrecht   *Dinner at the New Gene Cafe: How Genetic Engineering Is Changing What We Eat, How We Live, and the Global Politics of Food.* New York: St. Martin's Press, 2001.

Marion Nestle   *Food Politics: How the Food Industry Influences Nutrition and Health.* Berkeley: University of California Press, 2002.

J. Eric Oliver   *Fat Politics: The Real Story Behind America's Obesity Epidemic.* New York: Oxford University Press, 2006.

Barry Popkin   *The World Is Fat: The Fads, Trends, Policies, and Products That Are Fattening the Human Race.* New York: Penguin, 2009.

Janet Poppendieck   *Free for All: Fixing School Food in America.* Berkeley: University of California Press, 2010.

John Robbins   *Diet for a New America.* Walpole, NH: Stillpoint, 1987.

John Robbins   *The Food Revolution: How Your Diet Can Help Save Your Life and Our World.* 10th ed. San Francisco: Conari Press, 2011.

Eric Schlosser — *Fast Food Nation: The Dark Side of the All-American Meal*. New York: Harper Perennial, 2005.

Michele Simon — *Appetite for Profit: How the Food Industry Undermines Our Health and How to Fight Back*. New York: Nation Books, 2006.

Peter Singer and Jim Mason — *The Ethics of What We Eat: Why Our Food Choices Matter*. Emmaus, PA: Rodale, 2006.

Frances Sizer and Ellie Whitney — *Nutrition: Concepts and Controversies*. 11th ed. Belmont, CA: Thompson Higher Education, 2008.

Brian Wansink — *Mindless Eating: Why We Eat More than We Think*. New York: Bantam, 2006.

Ellie Whitney and Sharon Rady Rolfes — *Understanding Nutrition*. Belmont, CA: Wadsworth, 2011.

Walter C. Willett with Patrick J. Skerrett — *Eat, Drink, and Be Healthy: The Harvard Medical School Guide to Healthy Eating*. New York: Free Press, 2005.

Mark Winne — *Closing the Food Gap: Resetting the Table in the Land of Plenty*. Boston: Beacon Press, 2008.

Index